the • ENCYCLOPEDIA •
 O*of* rigami

the •ENCYCLOPEDIA•
Origami
of

THE COMPLETE, FULLY
ILLUSTRATED GUIDE TO THE
FOLDED PAPER ARTS

NICK ROBINSON

SEARCH PRESS

A QUARTO BOOK

Published in 2004 by Search Press Ltd
Wellwood
North Farm Road
Tunbridge Wells
Kent TN2 3DR
United Kingdom

Reprinted 2005, 2006

A catalogue record for this book is available
from the British Library.

Conceived, designed, and produced by
Quarto Publishing plc
The Old Brewery
6 Blundell Street
London N7 9BH

QUAR.EOGT

PROJECT EDITORS: Fiona Robertson, Liz Pasfield
ART EDITOR: Sheila Volpe
ASSISTANT ART DIRECTOR: Penny Cobb
COPY EDITOR: Fiona Robertson
DESIGNER: Karin Skånberg
ILLUSTRATOR: Nick Robinson
PHOTOGRAPHER: Martin Norris
PICTURE RESEARCH: Claudia Tate
INDEXER: Pamela Ellis

ART DIRECTOR: Moira Clinch
PUBLISHER: Piers Spence

Manufactured by Pica Digital, Singapore
Printed by SNP Leefung Printers Ltd, China

CONTENTS

INTRODUCTION

Even in this era of digital technology, a world without paper is unimaginable. Paper has existed for thousands of years, and since the printing revolution that followed Johannes Gutenberg's invention of movable type it has been the prime means of communicating and storing information. However, most people take paper for granted, viewing it purely as a medium for recording information or as a base upon which to create art. Origami – or paper folding – allows us to see paper itself as a medium for artistic expression. No tools, other than your hands and mind, are needed to create tiny works of art that give both the folder and the viewer pleasure that far exceeds the effort required to actually fold them.

The origins of origami are a subject of much conjecture, but it seems likely that as soon as paper was available, people will have folded it – playing with paper seems to be a natural human instinct. What is certain is that the earliest forms of origami came from the East – China and Japan – where the art was incorporated into spiritual life. Origami eventually reached the West through a number of possible routes, perhaps as part of a circus act.

The serious development of origami as a creative act, as opposed to reproducing traditional designs, was led in the 20th century by the Japanese master Akira Yoshizawa, who devised new techniques and, perhaps most importantly, a means of recording the folding sequences using diagrams. In the West, Lillian Oppenheimer and Robert Harbin were primarily responsible for encouraging the exchange of origami designs and ideas from the 1950s onwards.

Origami is now a worldwide activity, enjoyed by young and old of both sexes. The fact that you need no tools other than your hands, and

Beetle: Robert Lang has designed many beetles, all of which are modelled closely on specific insects.

Rose: This beautiful rose by Toshikazu Kawasaki is a modern classic and has inspired many variations.

Flowers: Emma Jane Griffiths created this flower display using a traditional model.

Racing car: Designed for an advertising agency by David Brill, this car uses several sheets to produce a clean finish.

that the raw material is found in abundance, means that it's a hobby that anyone can pick up, and standard symbols free the diagrams from dependence on language. Origami can be performed anywhere (it's perfect for amusing yourself on long journeys), in isolation and also in company – many folders enjoy communal sessions where the more experienced help the newcomers. Another reason why origami has spread so widely is that it is largely free from commercial restrictions. Folders are happy, in most cases, to release their designs for others to enjoy. There are clear origami ethics though: not to publish diagrams without permission and to acknowledge influence where it exists.

Anyone with an internet connection can quickly track down an almost endless supply of origami diagrams to fold from, and there are also many books available. However, most of these books and online diagrams assume that you are already familiar with the range of techniques and the symbols needed to follow the sequences. This book offers a thorough grounding in origami techniques, symbols and concepts, as well as a representative cross-section of the different types of designs, ranging from simple to complex. The examples have been carefully chosen to allow you to develop your folding abilities, and inexperienced folders should work though them in the order given to gain the necessary skills and technical knowledge required for the more challenging models. If you are more experienced and want to try out models without working through the introductory sections, the 'Reminder' information provided with some models will refresh your memory about techniques or bases discussed at the start of the book.

Shark: This superb design by John Montroll is folded from hand-coloured paper and foil by Mark Kennedy.

Origami has given me enormous pleasure over the past 20 years, as well as introducing me to many lifelong friends. I hope that this book will introduce you to the numerous delights of origami, and perhaps for you too provide the starting point for many future friendships.

Nick Robinson

GETTING STARTED

Many folders are perfectly content to use standard origami paper for all their models. They are, however, missing out on the amazingly rich diversity of paper types that is available to them. Not only is there a wide range of colours and patterns, but there are also various thicknesses, textures, and folding qualities to be found in different sorts of paper. To select the best type of paper for a model, you must consider the folding techniques required. Thicker, less flexible paper isn't suited to models where many layers overlap, or where narrow points will be created. Conversely, if you want to make a large display version of a fairly simple model, thicker paper will provide strength and longevity.

The most fundamental property required from paper used in origami is 'foldability' – the ability to take and retain a crease. Paper is made from fibres of wood, held together by a special glue known as 'size'. The fibres in some paper are of a uniform length, while in other paper the fibres are mixed. Some fibres will break cleanly when folded, others less so. Some fibres will be lined up in the same direction, others more randomly. All these factors will interact to determine the foldability of a particular sheet of paper.

There is no scientific formula that can be used to evaluate a sheet of paper; you simply have to fold it and judge the results. Some paper, such as newspaper and sugar paper, is practically useless for anything other than very simple, large designs. Bible paper (so-called because it is used to produce the pages of a bible) is both thin and very crisp – perfect for complex designs. Folders learn from experience to judge which types of paper are most suitable for a model.

TYPES OF PAPER

Many different varieties of commercial art paper, available from arts and crafts suppliers, are commonly used in origami. Some are even designed specifically for paper folding, and they range in availability and versatility. One important aspect to consider is whether both sides of the paper will be seen on the finished model. If they will, you may either need paper with the same colour on both sides (to hide what would otherwise have been white sections) or you may need contrasting colours. Here are some different types of paper you should investigate:

Foil paper More properly known as foil-backed paper, this has one shiny metallic surface, sometimes with an embossed pattern, and one plain white paper surface. You can buy foil paper in rolls and also in squares, ready for folding. Not all designs are suited to folding from foil, but for some complex or multi-layered designs this is the only practical way of quickly achieving a good result. Foil paper will help you to mould and shape a model into three dimensions, and it is a pragmatic way of achieving narrow points and closely packed layers. Any visible creases may look ugly, however, because the metallic surface breaks easily, revealing the white side. Many folders won't use foil paper, since it doesn't have the delicate look and feel of ordinary paper, and in some ways it allows you to cheat. If you fold a narrow point carelessly, you can still squeeze the foil together to achieve an apparently neat result.

Foil paper

Origami paper

Origami paper Origami paper is readily available these days, in a wide range of colours, sizes and patterns. You can buy packs of a variety of colours or of a single colour only (red paper is always useful at Christmas!). It is usually perfect for practising models and for producing smaller display versions. However, many models require a very large starting size of paper, or a non-square shape. Origami paper is also quite thin, making it unsuitable for larger models.

Wrapping paper Ordinary gift-wrapping paper is often plastic-based and therefore unsuitable for origami. However, plain brown wrapping paper is excellent for origami and you can buy it in large rolls, to cut down to size. Some folders like to use such plain paper because they believe it focuses attention on the model itself. A good origami design, they say, shouldn't rely upon exciting paper to enhance it. If you prefer a more colourful model, however, other types of wrapping paper, with attractive floral patterns, can be obtained from florists.

Washi paper Dating back to ancient times, washi is a high-quality paper handmade in Japan using stencils, woodblocks or silk screens. Sheets may have a single colour, but most washi paper is produced with typically Eastern patterns, and

seems almost like a length of cloth. The paper has an especially soft finish (you can feel the fibres), yet is also very strong.

Chiyogami paper Chiyogami is another type of Japanese paper, decorated with brightly coloured, woodblock-printed patterns. It was first produced in the late 18th century as a cheaper alternative to washi paper.

Photocopying paper Cheap and readily available, photocopying paper is perfect for many simpler models – especially modular designs where you need many sheets of a similar colour – although you will often have to cut the rectangular sheets down to square dimensions. It is also, of course, the paper of choice for making paper airplanes!

Chiyogami paper

Photocopying paper

Wrapping paper

Washi paper

Scrap paper If you are really desperate to fold, almost any paper will do, and you will be able to find free samples everywhere you go. Leaflets, posters, handouts, tickets, paper bags – the supply is almost unlimited. While perhaps not suitable for display purposes, you can pass many happy hours practising with scrap paper.

Paper money Money-folding is a specialized branch of origami. Banknotes are great for folding, as they are made to be hard-wearing and are crisp enough to hold a crease. Models designed with money usually allow some leeway in the sequence, since the proportions of notes vary. If the cheapest note of your currency is too expensive to use for folding, buy a sensible amount of the cheapest foreign note available at your local bank. Depending on the country of origin, you may get hundreds for a small amount of your own currency.

Paper money

Canson paper This is a type of fine-art paper that many folders enjoy using. It comes in a wide range of subtle colours, has a pleasing texture, and is suitable for making large models. It is also popular for use in the technique known as 'wet-folding', because it can be shaped while wet, and then left to set, holding its form. There are several similar brands of paper, which can usually be recognized quite easily by feeling and curling the paper. You will need to experiment with the different varieties so that you get a feel for those that are likely to work well.

NOTES FOR FOLDING

How to fold Folding is something we do frequently in our everyday lives, but in origami folding needs to be much more controlled and accurate. Every crease is important, especially the first. If you are folding a sheet of paper in half and leave a slight gap, the error will become proportionally larger as the paper is folded smaller. An inaccuracy like this may mean you are unable to complete a more complex design, and in any design it will prevent you from achieving a neat and attractive result. Take your time with every fold, lining it up carefully before flattening the crease. Once a crease is in place, it's still possible to adjust it, but the paper will soon become tired and make folding harder. Better to take a few seconds making sure the paper is correctly positioned before creasing than to spend minutes correcting a poorly positioned crease, or perhaps having to start again.

Following origami diagrams is an art in itself. They are usually designed to present the maximum of information in the minimum of steps. As well as recognizing the symbols used, get into the habit of checking the next step so you can see the results of the move. Be aware, however, that the next step may be rotated, turned over or drawn larger or smaller than the previous one. By reading the instructions carefully, you will (with luck) avoid unwanted or inaccurate creases. If you are new to origami, read the accompanying text even if you are confident that you understand the diagrams. There may be an extra clue there to help you.

Always turn the paper to make folds easier.

Another useful tip is to fold each design at least three times before moving on – each version will be neater and better than the last. As well as improving your finished result, you will be subconsciously memorizing the sequence. Experienced folders can reproduce hundreds of designs from memory, even very complex ones. They will have made no effort to memorize these models, but will simply have folded them so many times that the sequence has become second nature.

Where to fold As with most activities, a little preparation will make your folding easier. Find a quiet location, free from disturbances, with sufficient time to relax. Origami should not be rushed. Make sure you have clean hands and a clean, flat surface such as a table. Give yourself plenty of elbow room and leave space for the book or diagrams you are following.

Origami is a versatile activity. The majority of your folding time will be spent alone, but there is also great pleasure to be had from folding as part of a group. As well as the social aspect (many origami meetings produce soft drinks and cakes after every third model!) – there is no better way to complete a tricky design. If you reach a problem step while folding on your own, you can hit an origami brick wall. It may be that you can solve the problem with repeated efforts – and a good night's rest often works wonders. However, folding in company means your combined abilities will enable you to solve almost any problem.

Folders are by nature unselfish creatures who will devote as much time as is needed to help a fellow folder through a problem sequence.

CREATING YOUR OWN DESIGNS

People who are new to origami are often impressed by the folders who actually create the designs. However, they are not always as ingenious and artistic as might appear to be the case. While some designers start from scratch and plumb the depths of their imagination, others simply adapt existing ideas to form new concepts. The easiest way to come up with a new idea is to start by adjusting the folds of a simple design: make distances longer or shorter; alter some of the angles; add some extra creases; leave creases out. Try it and see what happens!

It's likely that at first you will rediscover designs that others have found before you. This doesn't matter. Every new design you find is part of a pathway towards future designs. Soon, your work will lose obvious influences and find a style of its own. While some folders are possessive about their creations, most realize that independent discovery is a normal part of origami. However, if you create a new model that owes a large part of its heritage to an existing design, it's common courtesy to mention the source of your inspiration on any diagrams you make.

Creativity has no rules, but the more techniques you have, the wider the range of subjects you can tackle. You don't have to follow accepted methods. Many innovations come from people who turn away from the work of other folders in search of uncharted territories. Most origami designs are based around folding in halves and quarters, creating 45- or 22.5-degree geometry. Instead of following this route, why not try working with 60-degree angles and folding into thirds (see pages 34 and 35)? The more approaches you explore, the more likely you are to produce really new ideas.

THE BASIC TECHNIQUES

When you listen to a virtuoso musician, his performance is a seamless flow of beautiful notes and melodies. However, even the most challenging piece of music can be broken down into individual techniques and phrases. It is the same with origami. A thorough understanding of basic techniques is essential if you are to progress towards the more challenging designs. These include understanding what the symbols are telling you as well as how to manipulate the paper.

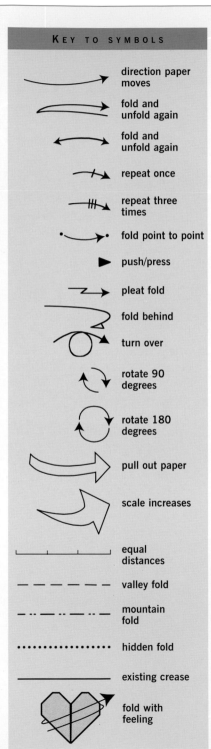

KEY TO SYMBOLS

	direction paper moves
	fold and unfold again
	fold and unfold again
	repeat once
	repeat three times
	fold point to point
	push/press
	pleat fold
	fold behind
	turn over
	rotate 90 degrees
	rotate 180 degrees
	pull out paper
	scale increases
	equal distances
	valley fold
	mountain fold
	hidden fold
	existing crease
	fold with feeling

BASIC FOLDS

At the heart of origami, there are only two folds: a valley fold and a mountain fold. You make them both (on opposite sides of the paper) whenever you make a crease. However, there are a number of instruction symbols that show you exactly where the crease is to lie. If you wish to progress in origami, you need to recognize all the standard symbols. There aren't many, although some artists draw them in slightly different ways.

Although many origami diagrams have text to accompany them, the beauty of origami symbols is that you don't need the text and so can follow diagrams written in any language. The symbols themselves should provide all the basic information you need. However, if there is text, you should also read it! Always 'read ahead' – look at the next step so you can see what you are aiming for.

Valley fold This fold can be made while the paper is flat on the table. The arrow shows the direction in which the paper moves. This type of crease is usually 'located', meaning you fold to a specific point, edge or crease.

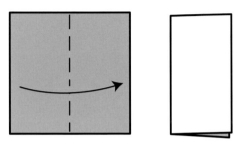

Valley fold and unfold Make a valley in the usual way, then unfold the paper to its position before the valley fold was made. Note the thinner line indicating the presence of a crease. Sometimes, a single line with an arrowhead at each end is used to indicate this move. While giving you essentially the same information, this doesn't tell you which side of the paper should move.

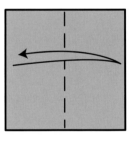

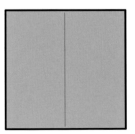

Mountain fold The paper folds underneath in some way so the fold must be made with the paper 'in the air'. Note the arrowhead, which is different to the valley-fold arrowhead. A mountain fold can be performed by turning the paper upside down and making a valley fold instead.

Mountain fold and unfold Complete a mountain fold, then unfold the paper to its original position.

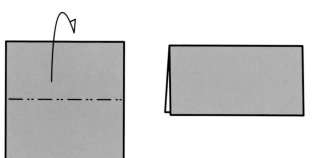

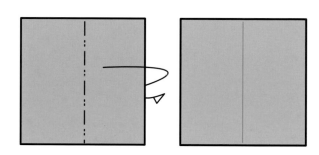

Repeat fold A fold indicated by the repeat arrow (in this case, taking a corner to the centre), should be repeated on a matching corner or side. Each notch on the arrow indicates a single repeat. This symbol is typically used to keep a diagram from becoming too busy or to avoid extra diagrams. Always check the next diagram if you are in doubt where to repeat.

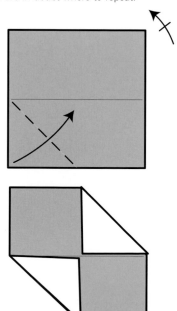

Fold point to point Plenty of folds do not have a clear location (such as a corner or intersection of creases) to fold to as they are made. In these cases, small dots are used to indicate the start and end of a fold.

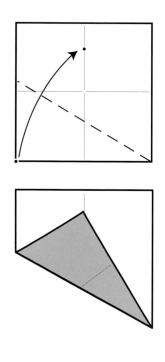

Fold equal amounts The rule next to the paper indicates that the creases are to divide the paper into equal thirds – although it doesn't actually tell you how to do this (see dividing a square into thirds, page 35). Note the alternative 'fold and unfold' symbol. Other rules can indicate quarters, sixths or fifths.

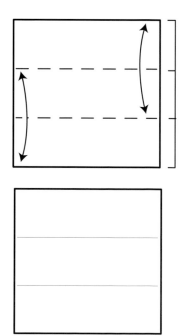

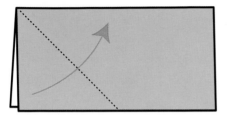

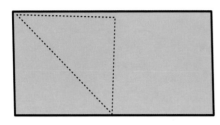

Hidden fold Sometimes a fold is made on layers of paper hidden inside the model. In this case a dotted or grey line is used to indicate where the fold takes place. It's important to read the text carefully at this stage.

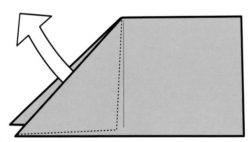

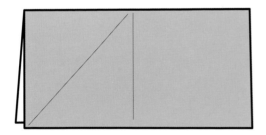

Pull out paper Some paper is released from within or underneath the model. Often, some degree of unfolding is necessary to do this. Never simply force the paper out.

Pleat on top A sequence of valley and mountain folds that forms a pleat. The upper layer moves on top of the lower layer forming a pleat in the paper. Part of the paper will then have two layers.

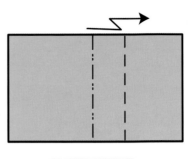

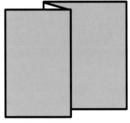

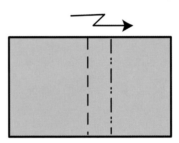

Pleat underneath Clearly, this is the same as the previous fold, but from a different perspective. Very often, you will see the pleat arrow and be expected to figure out where the paper goes yourself. Always check the next step if you're in doubt.

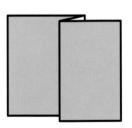

Fold with feeling Take special care whenever you see this sign. It means either the step needs very careful folding or you should fold gently. The symbol was inspired by the late American folder Michael Shall, who always insisted that we should 'fold with feeling'.

CHANGING ORIENTATION

With many steps, life is made easier if you alter the position of the paper. This may mean turning it over (like tossing a pancake) or rotating to a new position.

Turn over paper Lift the paper up and turn it over from right to left or left to right. If the arrow is rotated through 90 degrees, it indicates a turn from top to bottom or vice versa.

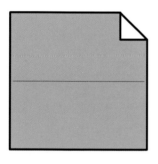

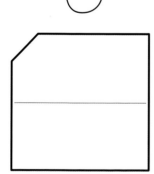

Rotate paper 90 degrees The arrows show the direction in which the paper is to be rotated.

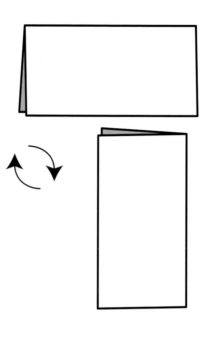

Rotate paper 180 degrees The arrows show the direction in which the paper is to be rotated. If an angle isn't indicated, match your paper to the next diagram.

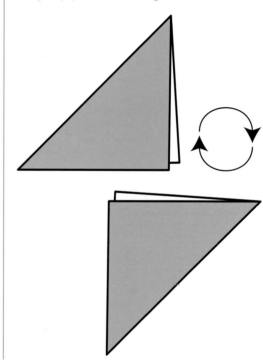

Scale increase As a sequence of folds progresses, the model usually gets smaller. In order to make the diagrams easy to read, at some stages the next step will be shown proportionally larger. Some diagrams simply do this without indicating, while others use a matching 'scale increase' symbol where appropriate.

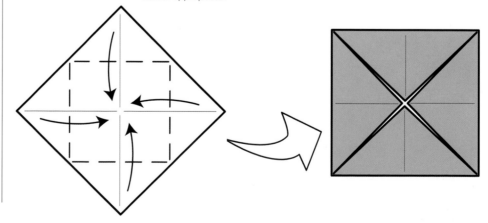

REVERSE FOLDING

This technique often confuses beginners to origami, but, if you analyse it carefully, it is perfectly straightforward. The name comes from the fact that a section of the paper reverses from valley to mountain or vice versa. It is perhaps used most frequently to form feet or beaks, but also has many other uses. The process of adding necessary creases before making a fold is known as 'pre-creasing'.

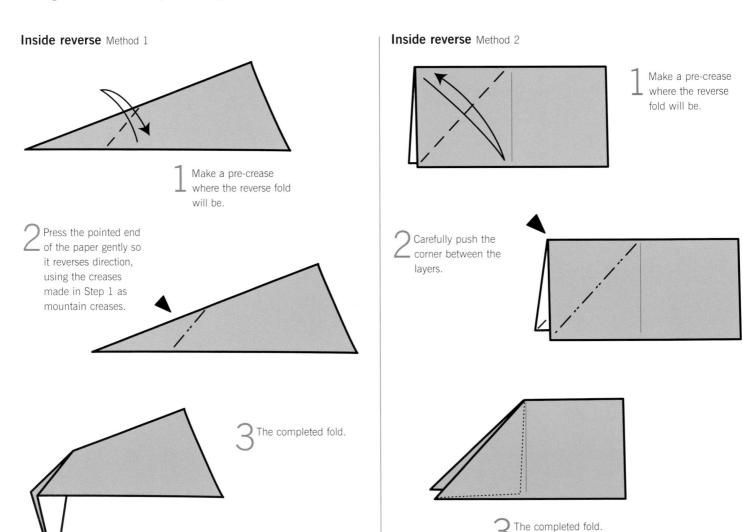

Inside reverse Method 1

1 Make a pre-crease where the reverse fold will be.

2 Press the pointed end of the paper gently so it reverses direction, using the creases made in Step 1 as mountain creases.

3 The completed fold.

Inside reverse Method 2

1 Make a pre-crease where the reverse fold will be.

2 Carefully push the corner between the layers.

3 The completed fold.

Outside reverse

1 Make a pre-crease where the reverse fold will be.

2 Peel apart the papers and wrap them around.

3 The completed fold.

Double reverse

1 Form a pleat to mark the position of the reverses.

2 Unfold the pleat.

3 Sink the point inside the layers.

4 Reverse the inner point back out using the existing creases.

5 The completed fold.

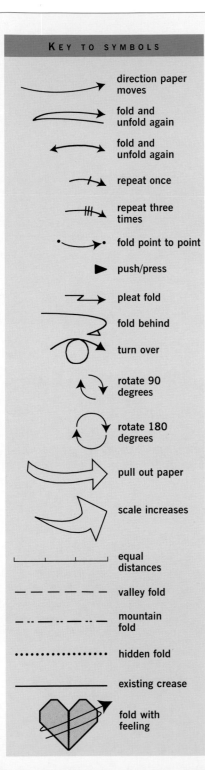

KEY TO SYMBOLS	
	direction paper moves
	fold and unfold again
	fold and unfold again
	repeat once
	repeat three times
	fold point to point
	push/press
	pleat fold
	fold behind
	turn over
	rotate 90 degrees
	rotate 180 degrees
	pull out paper
	scale increases
	equal distances
– – – – –	valley fold
– · – · – · –	mountain fold
· · · · · · · · ·	hidden fold
————	existing crease
	fold with feeling

ESSENTIAL SEQUENCES

Certain sequences of folds occur regularly throughout origami and have been given names to make life easier. They allow us to give broad instructions that save time and detail. To break these instructions (and other techniques) down into individual steps every time they were used would mean that origami diagrams would be much longer. By using this form of 'shorthand' we can present a lot of information in a few words.

It is important not only that you can perform these sequences, but also that you understand exactly what is happening. To achieve this, you should unfold and refold each sequence until you are clear exactly how the paper is behaving, which flaps move to where and if you need to take extra care at any stage. Some sequences put stress on the paper and careless folding can cause a rip!

RABBIT'S EAR

This sequence folds two adjacent sides together, pinching the corner into a flap that can be flattened to either side. It doesn't especially resemble the ear of a rabbit, but that's what it's called. The move appears in various forms throughout origami and is a very useful technique. Here, it is shown formed from one side of a square. If you perform the move on both sides of the paper, you will create a fish base (see page 30).

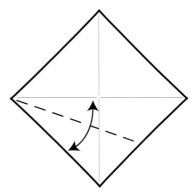

1 Start with a square, creased on both diagonals. Fold the lower left edge to meet the horizontal diagonal. Crease and unfold.

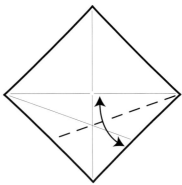

2 Repeat the fold on the lower right edge. These creases need only be made as far as the vertical diagonal, but are shown here complete for ease of folding.

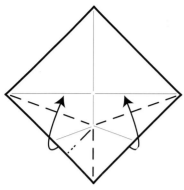

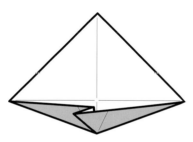

3 Now fold in both sides together, forming a valley fold in the centre. The small mountain fold forms itself as you start to flatten the point later.

4 Here is the move in progress: the triangular flap is being flattened to the left.

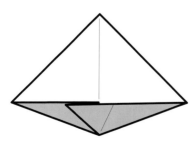

5 Fully flattened – the completed rabbit's ear.

DOUBLE RABBIT'S EAR

This is an elegant sequence that narrows part of a flap while at the same time changing its angle. This fold doesn't at first seem related to the rabbit's ear, but if you open up the flap after performing the technique, you'll see rabbit's-ear creases on either side.

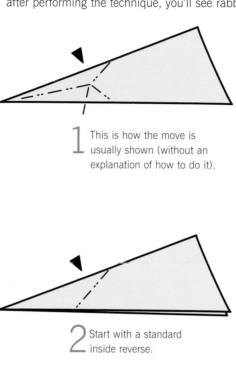

1 This is how the move is usually shown (without an explanation of how to do it).

2 Start with a standard inside reverse.

3 Crease the flap in half.

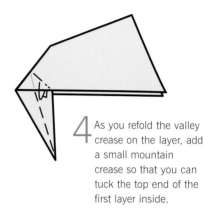

4 As you refold the valley crease on the layer, add a small mountain crease so that you can tuck the top end of the first layer inside.

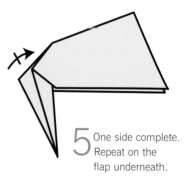

5 One side complete. Repeat on the flap underneath.

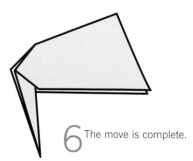

6 The move is complete.

CRIMP

A crimp allows you to create a change of angle in a strip or pointed flap. The paper that is 'lost' in the fold lies either inside or outside the rest of the paper, determining whether it is an inside or outside crimp. Once you understand the procedure, crimps can be made directly into the paper, but for accuracy it is usual to pre-crease them. To do this, fold all layers with a mountain and valley fold as shown. It doesn't matter which is which, since you need to reverse the directions of half the creases anyway.

Inside crimp

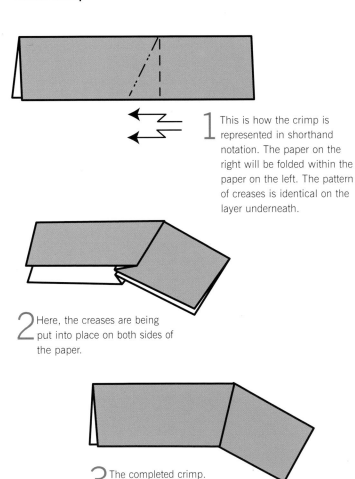

1 This is how the crimp is represented in shorthand notation. The paper on the right will be folded within the paper on the left. The pattern of creases is identical on the layer underneath.

2 Here, the creases are being put into place on both sides of the paper.

3 The completed crimp.

Outside crimp

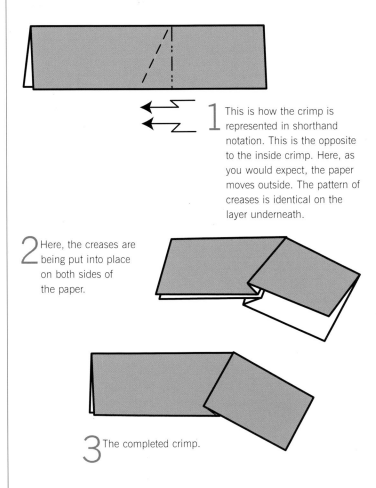

1 This is how the crimp is represented in shorthand notation. This is the opposite to the inside crimp. Here, as you would expect, the paper moves outside. The pattern of creases is identical on the layer underneath.

2 Here, the creases are being put into place on both sides of the paper.

3 The completed crimp.

PETAL

One of the classic sequences in origami, a petal involves folding several creases at the same time to produce a neat and unexpected result. While experienced folders can make a petal fold directly into the paper, it's much easier if you add the necessary pre-creases first.

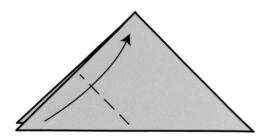

1 This example begins from a waterbomb base (see page 29). Fold the bottom-left corner to the top corner.

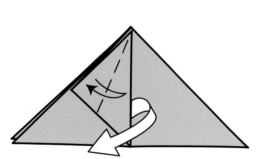

2 Fold the top two shorter edges to the centre crease, then unfold back to Step 1.

3 You now have all the creases you need to make the petal fold. Squash the flap symmetrically in half.

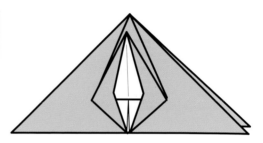

4 Using the horizontal crease as a hinge, swing the lower point upwards. The lower raw edges will start to fold inwards.

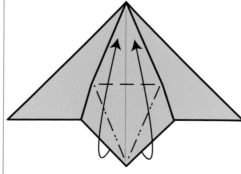

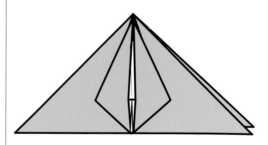

5 Here is the move in progress.

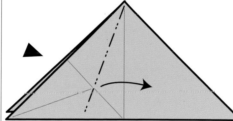

6 And completed. Unfold and refold until you understand what is happening. If you do this to each of the flaps, you will form a frog base.

SINK

A sink is typically applied to a 'closed' corner point (i.e. one formed with folded edges only). The section of paper above the sink line disappears completely into the paper. Like reverse folding, this is a technique that often confuses beginners, but it shouldn't present a problem if you pre-crease accurately and fold carefully. The hard part is to get the creases inside the sink to lie neatly. If you are folding foil paper, this can be almost impossible. (You may be lucky enough to come across a double sink, where the paper goes in, then comes partially out again!)

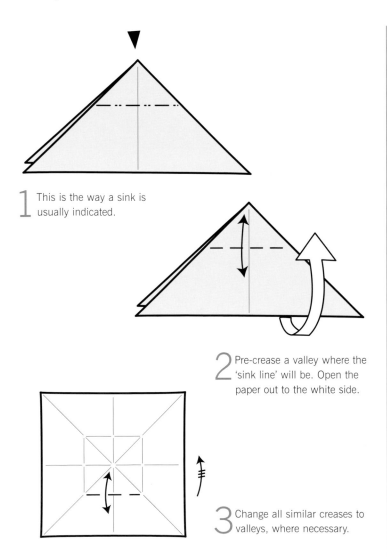

1 This is the way a sink is usually indicated.

2 Pre-crease a valley where the 'sink line' will be. Open the paper out to the white side.

3 Change all similar creases to valleys, where necessary.

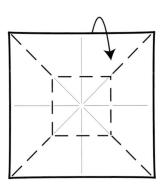

4 Form the paper into a 3-D shape, turning it upside down.

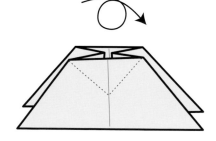

5 Start to press in the centre. Whether a crease on the outside is a valley or a mountain, make sure that it is the opposite on the inside. So, for example, the outside section from the corner is a mountain, but as it passes the sink line it becomes a valley. Fold carefully and don't force the paper.

6 Complete the sink.

SQUASH

This term describes the technique of lifting a double layer of paper and squashing the layers apart as you flatten them. If you can't see anything to line up with the fold, you may need to turn the paper upside down before the final flatten. You should initially pre-crease both creases involved (the mountain crease can go either way during pre-creasing, but the valley crease should be pre-creased as a valley). With practice, you can sometimes form squashes directly, without pre-creasing. No method of forming a squash is better than another, it depends entirely on what the origami design requires.

Method 1

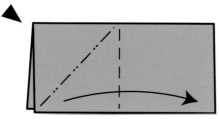

1 This is how the squash is shown. Swing the paper over on the valley, while pressing the corner shown.

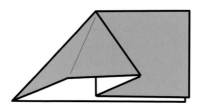

2 The fold in progress.

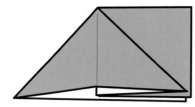

3 With luck, the paper will settle in this position.

Method 2

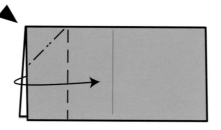

1 This is almost the same as the first example, but it's applied to a shorter flap of paper.

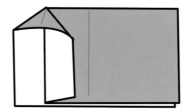

2 The fold in progress.

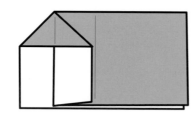

3 This is the completed fold.

Method 3

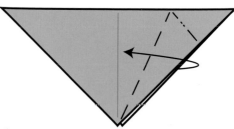

1 This looks quite different to the other two squash examples, but the same principles apply. In this instance you may only want to pre-crease the valley fold, since you're not sure where the other crease will lie.

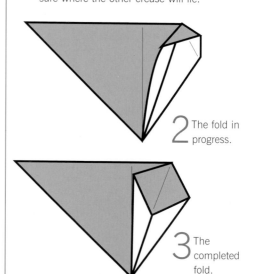

2 The fold in progress.

3 The completed fold.

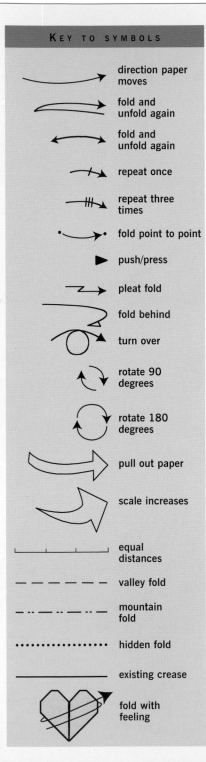

KEY TO SYMBOLS

direction paper moves

fold and unfold again

fold and unfold again

repeat once

repeat three times

fold point to point

push/press

pleat fold

fold behind

turn over

rotate 90 degrees

rotate 180 degrees

pull out paper

scale increases

equal distances

valley fold

mountain fold

hidden fold

existing crease

fold with feeling

BASES

When creative people began to analyse origami in the early part of the last century, they noticed that several designs began with an identical sequence of folds. These came to be known as bases and were given names that usually reflected a design commonly made from them. Thus a base that could be made into a fish was called a fish base and so forth. One exception is the preliminary base, so-called because it is a starting point for many different designs.

The beauty of a base is that it forms a starting point for you to be creative. Faced with a plain square, people often find it difficult to progress, but given (for example) a bird base, they can play with the many possibilities and perhaps come up with a new design. Needless to say, a thorough grounding in traditional bases will help you towards success in origami.

KITE BASE

Probably the simplest of origami bases, the kite allows you to create uncomplicated designs, such as pecking birds and owls. Although this is a very simple base, it still needs folding carefully and accurately. It's interesting to see how this base is developed into a fish base (see page 30).

BLINTZ BASE

This base is formed by folding each corner of a square to the centre. To find the centre, add any two of the 'union jack' creases (diagonal or side-to-opposite creases). However, folding to the centre can sometimes lead to inaccuracies: it's always easier to fold to an edge rather than a crease line. The method opposite is an excellent way of folding a very clean (minimally creased) blintz base. The word blintz itself comes from a way of folding Jewish pastry.

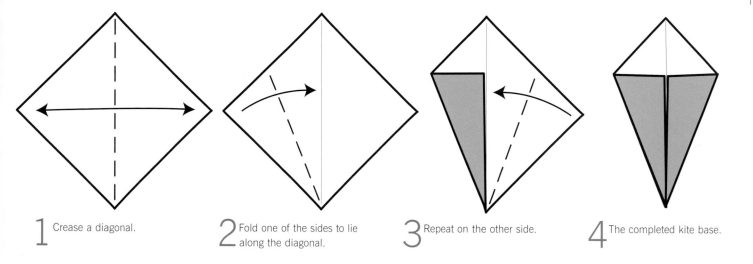

1 Crease a diagonal.

2 Fold one of the sides to lie along the diagonal.

3 Repeat on the other side.

4 The completed kite base.

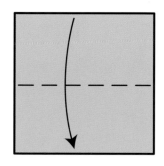

1 Fold a square in half.

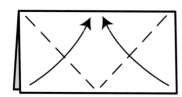

2 Fold the two shorter edges to meet the top edge.

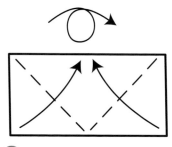

3 Turn the paper over and repeat the last step.

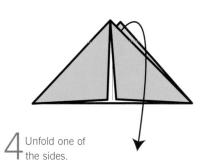

4 Unfold one of the sides.

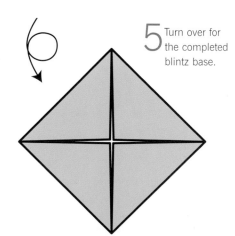

5 Turn over for the completed blintz base.

PRELIMINARY BASE

This is called the preliminary base because it is the starting position for many origami designs. It's well worth studying this base carefully so you can see how a precise combination of valley and mountain creases is needed to form it. If any of these creases are made incorrectly, it simply won't work. This base also exemplifies an origami technique that produces many points where there were few. The four corners of the square produce nine (count them!) points with which you can work.

Method 1

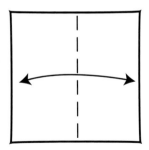

1 Fold a square in half from side to side, crease and unfold.

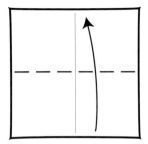

2 Fold the square in half from bottom to top.

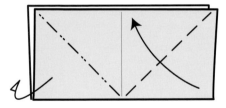

3 Fold the bottom-right corner to the top centre. Turn over and repeat the fold on the other side (shown here as a mountain fold).

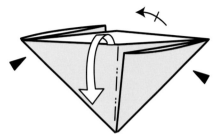

4 Open the layers evenly and press the sides together, in effect squashing the model in half.

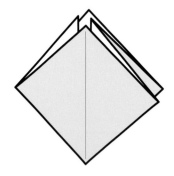

5 A preliminary base is formed.

Method 2

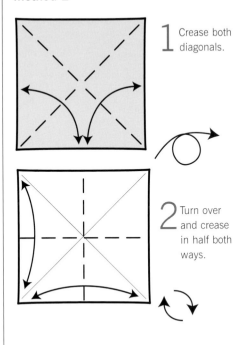

1 Crease both diagonals.

2 Turn over and crease in half both ways.

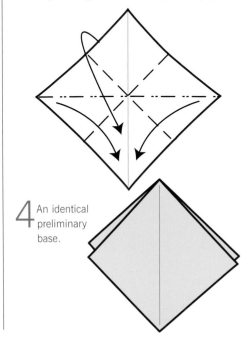

3 Rotate the paper through 45 degrees. Use only existing creases to collapse the paper.

4 An identical preliminary base.

WATERBOMB BASE

It's hard to see at first, but the crease pattern for the preliminary base is the same one needed for the waterbomb base. This means you can take a preliminary base and flip it inside out to form a waterbomb base. However, the two methods shown for the preliminary base can also be easily adapted to form the waterbomb base directly.

Method 1

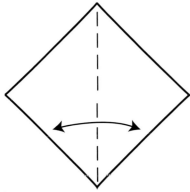

1 Fold a square from corner to opposite corner, crease and unfold.

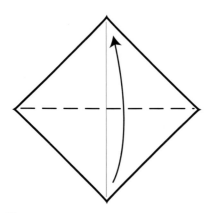

2 Fold in half from bottom to top.

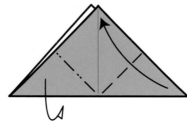

3 Fold the bottom-right corner to the top centre. Turn over and repeat the fold on the other side (shown here as a mountain fold).

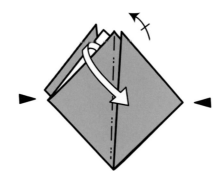

4 Open the layers evenly and press the sides together, in effect squashing in half.

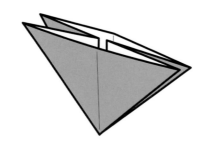

5 A waterbomb base is formed.

Method 2

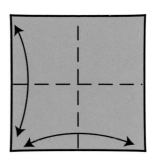

1 Crease the square in half both ways.

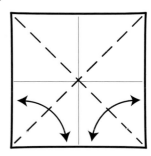

2 Turn over and crease both diagonals.

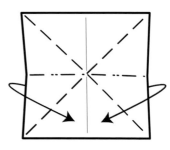

3 Use only existing creases to collapse the paper.

4 An identical waterbomb base.

FISH BASE

This base produces an extended diamond shape with two smaller flaps at the centre. It is commonly folded in half to form a kite shape with two layers. The tips of these layers can easily be folded over to form the fins of a simple fish.

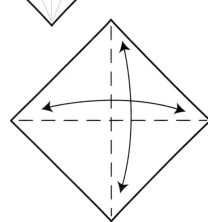

1 Crease both diagonals from the white side.

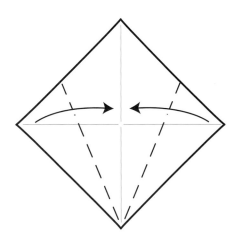

2 Fold the two lower raw edges to the vertical centre crease.

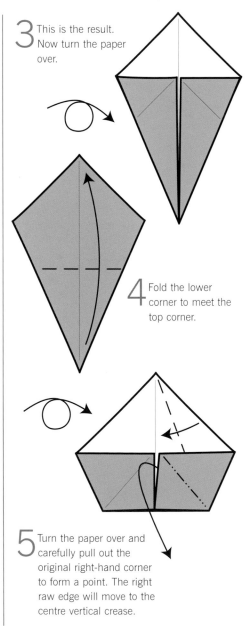

3 This is the result. Now turn the paper over.

4 Fold the lower corner to meet the top corner.

5 Turn the paper over and carefully pull out the original right-hand corner to form a point. The right raw edge will move to the centre vertical crease.

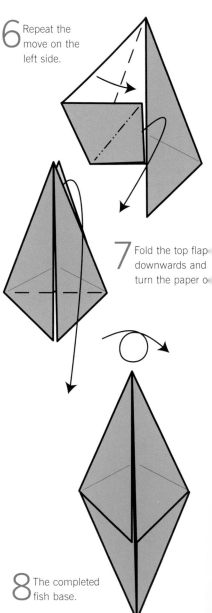

6 Repeat the move on the left side.

7 Fold the top flap downwards and turn the paper o[ver]

8 The completed fish base.

BIRD BASE

A bird base is so-called due to the number of birds that can easily be folded from it. The bird base has four narrow points at one end and a blunter one at the opposite end. Its crease pattern (right) shows a perfect and beautiful symmetry.

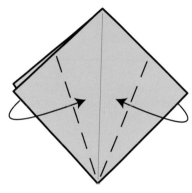

1 Start with a preliminary base, coloured side outwards. Fold two outer flaps in to the vertical centre crease.

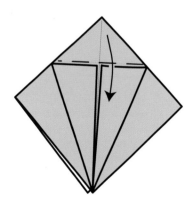

2 Fold the top triangular flap downwards.

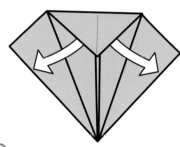

3 Pull the side flaps out from beneath the top flap.

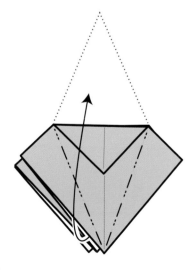

4 Lift the corner of the first layer of paper at the bottom and swing it upwards, using the top of the triangular flap as a hinge.

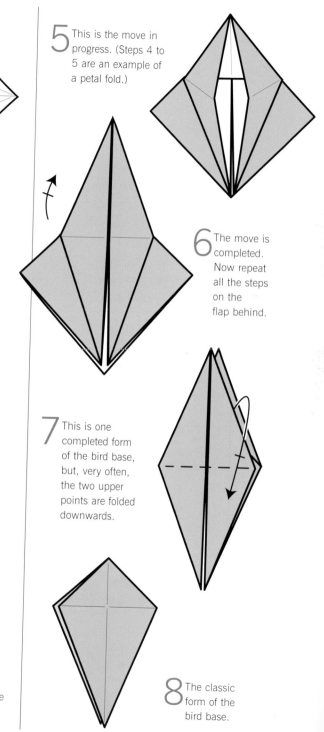

5 This is the move in progress. (Steps 4 to 5 are an example of a petal fold.)

6 The move is completed. Now repeat all the steps on the flap behind.

7 This is one completed form of the bird base, but, very often, the two upper points are folded downwards.

8 The classic form of the bird base.

3 Refold

5 You ca
Repeat
all step

M

J
c
c a
a o
r h
h p
p
p r r
r
a

Meth

1

BEGINNER PROJECTS

Here are some designs carefully selected to introduce you to the symbols and moves that you will need for simple models. They will also show you a small part of the rich diversity of subjects you can fold with paper. To get the best from this book, work through this chapter before tackling any of the more advanced projects!

WATERBOMB FISH

Design by various creators

8 STEPS

With one extra crease, the humble waterbomb base transforms into an angelfish. With a couple more, it becomes a traditional fish. These are the types of fold that people discover through playing with the paper, looking for logical folds to make, and using their imagination. With many tens of thousands of folders in the world, it follows that several people are likely to rediscover the same design. While it's always disappointing to find out that your wonderful creation isn't quite as unique as you had hoped, you shouldn't let this upset you too much. The idea came from your own creativity and it's not surprising that you should share similar approaches with other people.

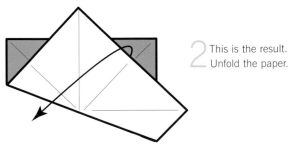

Paper size:
7 in. (18 cm) square
Finished waterbomb fish:
4 in. (10 cm) high

WATERBOMB BASE
REMINDER

1. Fold in half both ways.

2. Turn over and add both diagonals.

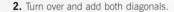

3. Refold using existing creases.

4. Complete.

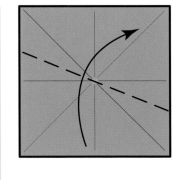

1 Start with a waterbomb base (see reminder panel, left), folded with the coloured side outwards. Unfold and turn to the coloured side. Make a fold that passes through the centre of the square, arranged so that the lower vertical crease meets the upper right diagonal crease.

2 This is the result. Unfold the paper.

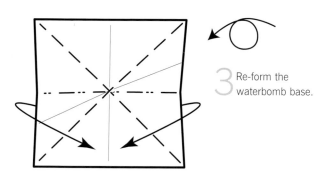

3 Re-form the waterbomb base.

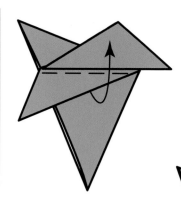

6 To continue, fold the large, upper flap to the right, so that the raw edges lie horizontally and pass over the nose of the fish.

4 Swivel the upper triangle to the right and upwards, while keeping the lower triangle still. You're aiming to fold on the crease you made in Step 1.

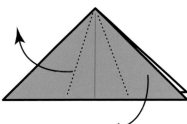

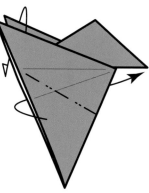

7 Then fold the tail fin up over the same flap. Repeat the last two steps on the side underneath.

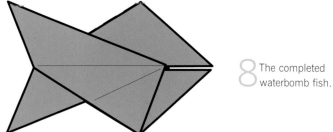

8 The completed waterbomb fish.

5 Here's the result, a simple, elegant angelfish.

FOLDER'S TIP

Form interesting patterns by arranging several fish together on a larger sheet. Shown here are a collection of angelfish and a collage of waterbomb fish slotted together.

TARUMPTY TUM TUM

Design by Siero Takekawa

9 STEPS

This model is by the Japanese master of simple origami designs, Takekawa. If balanced on one end, with the heavier side upwards, it will turn a full somersault when tipped over. You can play an origami game by showing friends how the model tips, then asking them to try for themselves. The trick is to place the model with its lighter end upwards; it won't somersault from that position and only the most observant people will guess why.

Paper size:
18 cm (7 in.) square
Finished model:
9 cm (3½ in.) high

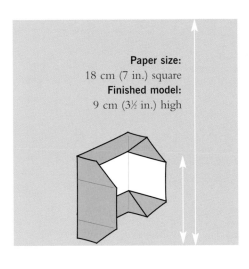

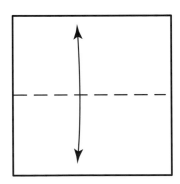

1 Start with a square of paper. Fold it in half from top to bottom, then unfold.

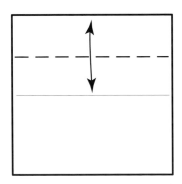

2 Fold the upper side to the centre, crease and unfold.

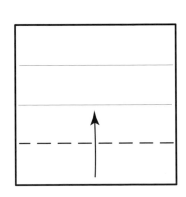

3 Fold the lower side to the centre, and leave it in place.

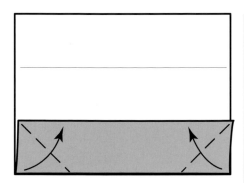

4 Fold in two corners to line up along the coloured raw edge.

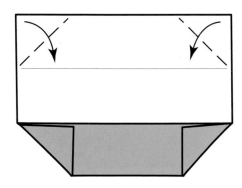

5 Repeat with the two original corners, folding to the crease.

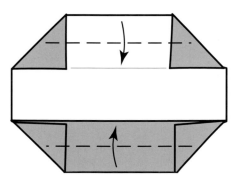

6 Fold the top and bottom sections in half. Hold the corners in place so they don't pop out as you fold.

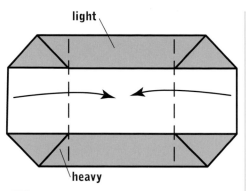

light

heavy

7 The heavier side, with extra layers of paper, is marked here. Fold the side ends to meet in the centre. You're folding on hidden layers and will be able to feel where the paper naturally folds.

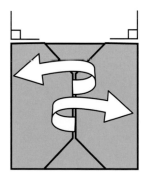

8 Open out these two flaps so they are at right angles to the central section.

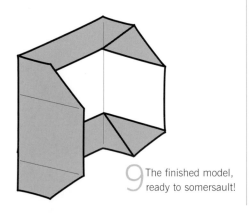

9 The finished model, ready to somersault!

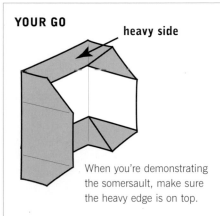

CHALLENGE

There's an ongoing Tarumpty Tum Tum challenge in origami. Models are lined up so that one knocks over another. The aim is to topple the greatest number with a single push. The current world record is 123. Can you beat it? Remember that one topple could be used to start the next two topples.

YOUR GO

heavy side

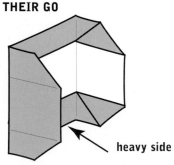

When you're demonstrating the somersault, make sure the heavy edge is on top.

THEIR GO

heavy side

Then casually set up the model with the light edge on top, so that it won't tip over.

PRINTER'S HAT

Traditional design

11 STEPS

Very few origami designs have a practical function. This hat is one of them; it was used for many years by printers to keep their heads free from ink stains. It can be created from most rectangular shapes, but is especially effective made from newspaper, which can be fitted to most heads. Alter Step 5 to adjust the size.

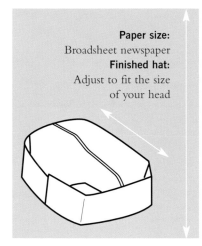

Paper size:
Broadsheet newspaper
Finished hat:
Adjust to fit the size
of your head

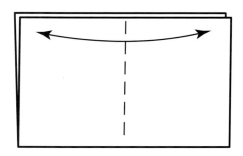

1 Start with a double sheet of newspaper (or other paper) folded in half. Fold the short edges together, crease and unfold.

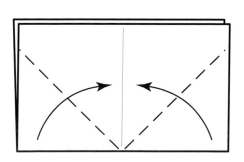

2 Fold each half of the lower (folded) edge to the centre crease.

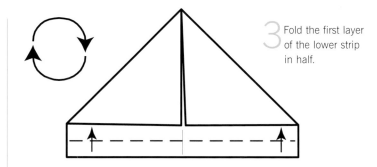

3 Fold the first layer of the lower strip in half.

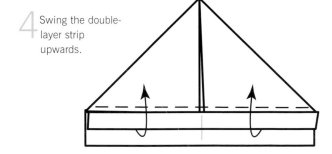

4 Swing the double-layer strip upwards.

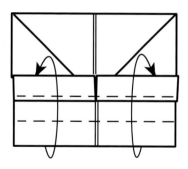

7 Fold the layer up and tuck it into the pocket.

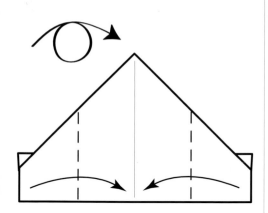

5 Turn the paper over and fold in the sides to the centre. (Fold slightly less for a larger head.)

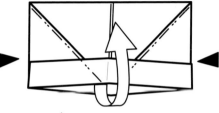

8 You can use the paper as a soldier's cap at this stage. Open the lower edges in opposite directions, while pressing in at the sides.

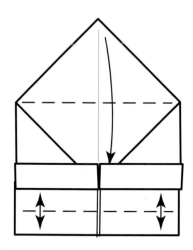

6 Tuck the upper triangle behind the thin layers. Fold the lower strip in half.

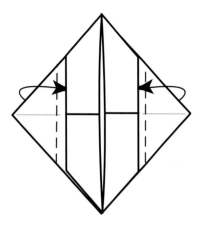

9 If you continue pressing, the paper flattens into a square shape. Tuck the side flaps into the pockets.

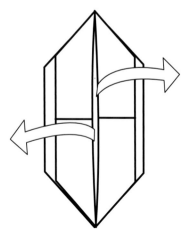

10 Open the layers from within and shape the hat.

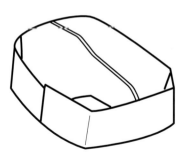

11 The printer's hat is complete and ready for use.

FOLDER'S TIP

If your head is especially large, you may need to tape two sheets of newspaper together! With practice you'll be able to adjust the dimensions to make hats for any size of head.

ROCKING NUN

Traditional design

7 STEPS

A few folders prefer to work with circular paper. This may seem a little pointless, because as soon as you fold in four opposite sides of a circle, you have a square. The idea, however, is to fold simple designs that utilize the circle's curves in some way. This design is also an action model (in other words, it isn't just a static model, but does something).

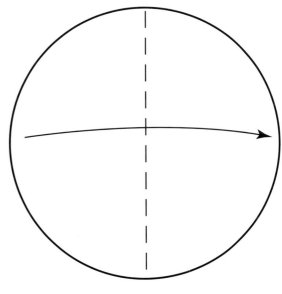

Paper size:
18 cm (7 in.) diameter
Finished nun:
13 cm (5 in.) high

OUTSIDE REVERSE
REMINDER

1. Pre-crease the paper.

2. Open both sides, flipping the point inside out.

3. Complete.

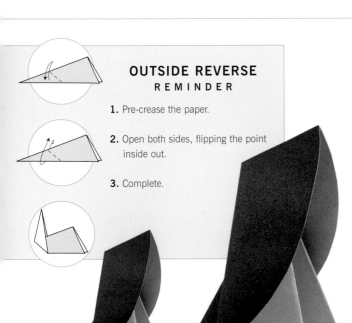

1 Start with a circle (ideally black on one side and white on the other) and fold it in half.

2 Fold over both layers, as shown.

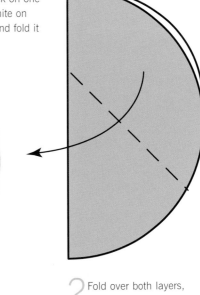

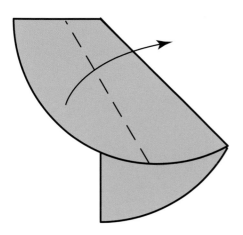

3 Fold back a section, to match the next diagram.

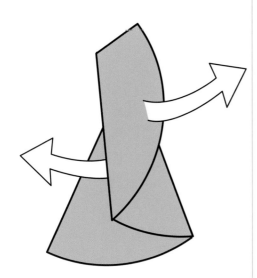

4 Unfold the last two moves.

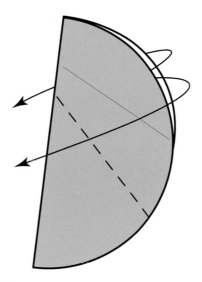

5 Make an outside-reverse fold (see reminder panel, left), using the lower of the two creases you've made.

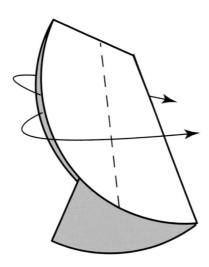

6 Make a second reverse fold using the other crease.

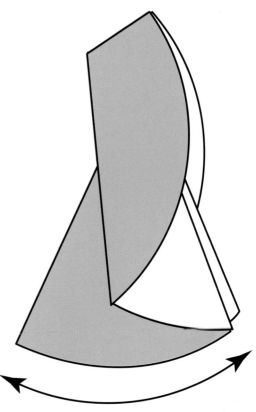

7 The completed nun, ready to rock!

CHALLENGE

Can you design a simple model from circular paper? Remember, if you make too many creases the paper becomes just another square. Your design needs to use the curved edge of your paper.

FUSE BOX

Design by Tomoko Fuse

10 STEPS

Tomoko Fuse caused a minor revolution in origami when she unveiled her system for making boxes from several sheets of paper. The seemingly endless series of fascinating containers (often with perfectly fitting lids), made with three, four, five, six, eight or twelve sides, proved her to be a major creative talent. This box is one of the simplest of her repertoire, and a classic of economy and efficiency. You may feel that you need an extra pair of hands towards the end, but the model is perfectly achievable. You'll need four squares, two each of two colours (or four of different colours).

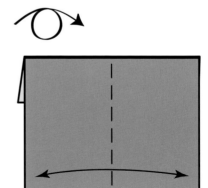

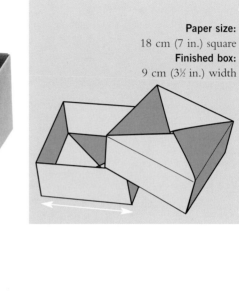

Paper size:
18 cm (7 in.) square
Finished box:
9 cm (3½ in.) width

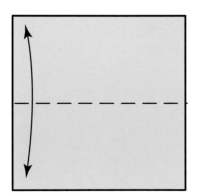

1 Start with a square, lighter side upwards, and crease in half.

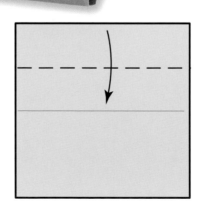

2 Fold the top edge to the centre crease. Turn the paper over.

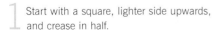

3 Fold in half from side to side, crease and unfold. Turn the paper over again.

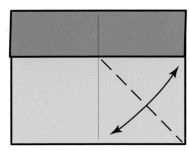

4 Crease the lower right diagonal and unfold.

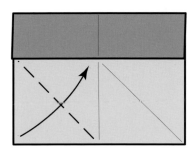

5 Fold the lower left corner to the centre.

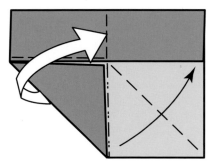

6 Use the creases shown to form the paper into three dimensions. You'll need to pinch the upper third of the centre crease into a valley.

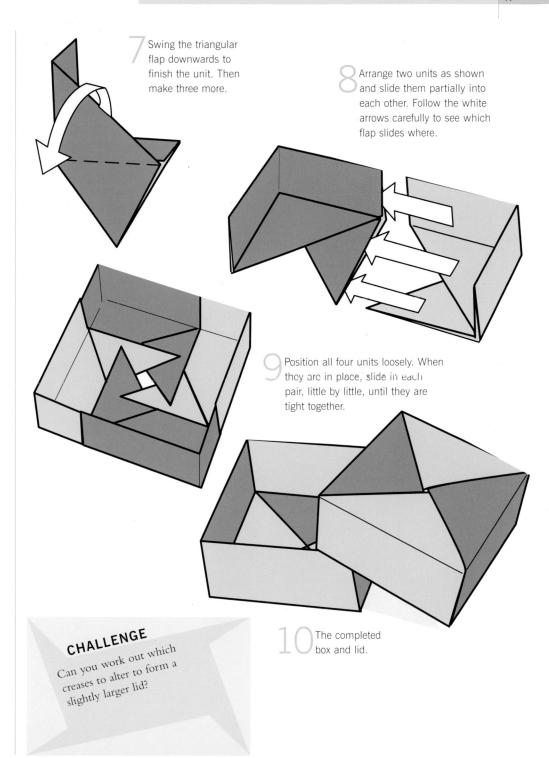

7 Swing the triangular flap downwards to finish the unit. Then make three more.

8 Arrange two units as shown and slide them partially into each other. Follow the white arrows carefully to see which flap slides where.

9 Position all four units loosely. When they arc in place, slide in each pair, little by little, until they are tight together.

10 The completed box and lid.

CHALLENGE
Can you work out which creases to alter to form a slightly larger lid?

BAGGI'S BOX

Design by Giuseppi Baggi
11 STEPS

Baggi was a highly creative American folder
of the early 1960s. This is one of his
classic designs, a delightfully simple yet
very practical box. You can make it
from a rectangle of almost any
proportions and can start with the
paper laid either lengthways
or sideways.

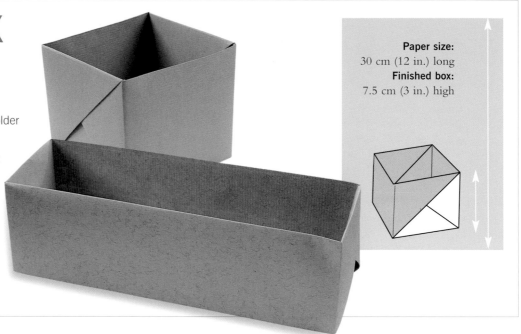

Paper size:
30 cm (12 in.) long
Finished box:
7.5 cm (3 in.) high

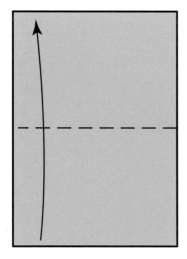

1 Starting with a rectangle, fold the lower
short edge to the upper edge.

2 Fold the upper raw
edge to the lower edge,
crease and unfold.
Repeat the move
behind, then unfold
from underneath, back
to the rectangle.

3 Fold in the lower
corners to meet the
first horizontal
crease. Turn over
the paper.

4 Form a vertical
crease that starts
at the lower left
corner. Repeat on
the right-hand
side.

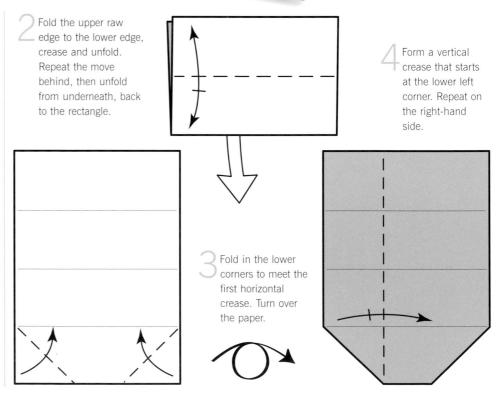

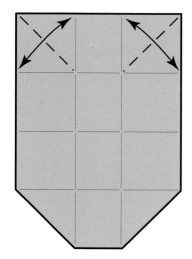

5 Crease two diagonals on the upper corners.

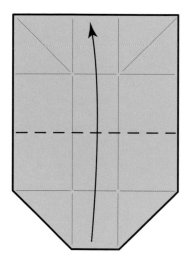

6 Fold in half upwards, using an existing crease.

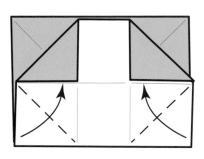

7 Fold over the two lower (double-thickness) corners.

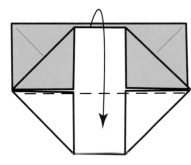

8 Fold the upper flap down over the two corners.

9 Gently lift the top edge and open the model into three dimensions.

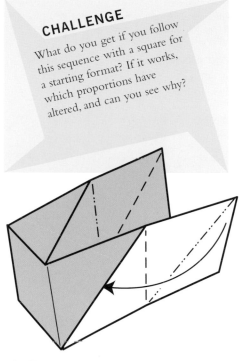

10 Use existing creases to carefully tuck the corners into the pockets.

11 The completed box. To make the longer format box, start with the paper rotated by 90 degrees and follow the same sequence.

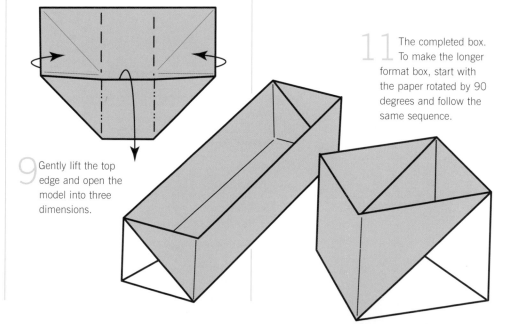

GRASSHOPPER

Design by Gay Gross

5 STEPS

Simple action models can be much harder to create than complicated ones. Capturing the form of a living subject as well as its movement requires true empathy with both nature and origami. This design is best made from crisp paper, so you can give it a good tap to start the movement without damaging it.

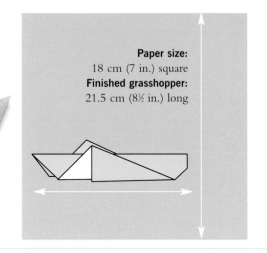

Paper size:
18 cm (7 in.) square
Finished grasshopper:
21.5 cm (8½ in.) long

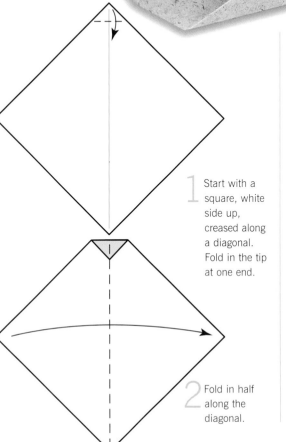

1 Start with a square, white side up, creased along a diagonal. Fold in the tip at one end.

2 Fold in half along the diagonal.

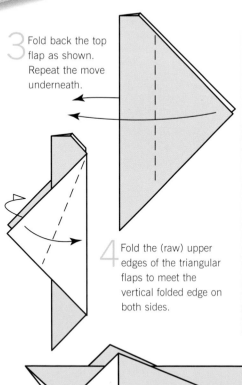

3 Fold back the top flap as shown. Repeat the move underneath.

4 Fold the (raw) upper edges of the triangular flaps to meet the vertical folded edge on both sides.

CHALLENGE

How high can your grasshopper jump?

5 The grasshopper is ready for action. Make it jump with a smart tap on the tail end. You will need to practise to perfect the action.

SAIL ON THE HORIZON

Design by Nick Robinson

6 STEPS

A relatively unexplored area of origami uses the two colours of origami paper to depict a scene. Here the silhouette of a sailing-boat on the horizon at dusk is evoked.

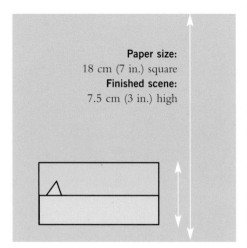

Paper size:
18 cm (7 in.) square
Finished scene:
7.5 cm (3 in.) high

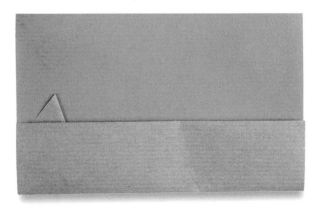

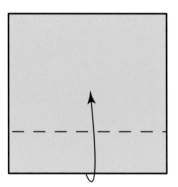

1 Fold over about one-quarter of the sheet.

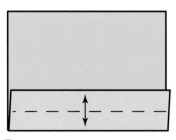

2 Crease this flap in half.

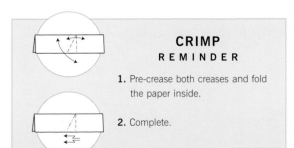

CRIMP
REMINDER

1. Pre-crease both creases and fold the paper inside.

2. Complete.

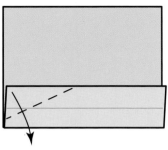

3 Fold over a corner (note the start and end points carefully).

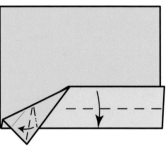

4 At one end make a crimp (see reminder panel, left), as you fold the raw edge downwards.

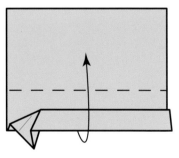

5 Fold over about one-third of the paper.

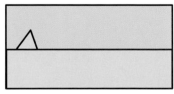

6 The completed scene.

HEADLANDS

Design by Tony O'Hare

7 STEPS

This is another example of the contrasting-colour technique, this time from Welshman O'Hare, who creates a coastal scene of cliffs and beaches.

Paper size:
18 cm (7 in.) long
Finished scene:
16.5 cm (6½ in.) high

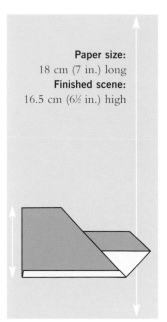

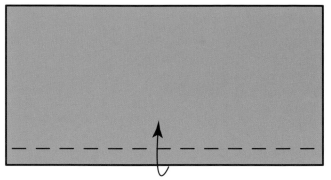

1 Start with a 2 x 1 rectangle (this is a rectangle whose length is twice its width), coloured side upwards. Fold up a small strip at the bottom edge.

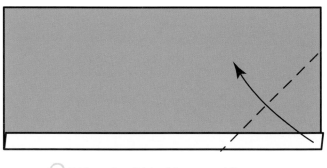

2 Fold over two-thirds of the paper at the lower right-hand edge. It doesn't have to be exact.

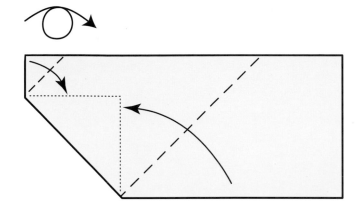

3 Turn over the paper. Fold the lower and left-hand raw edges to line up with the hidden edge (underneath).

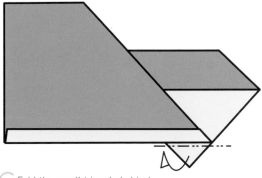

6 Fold the small triangle behind.

4 This is the result. Turn over the paper again.

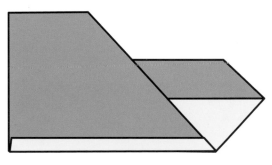

7 Complete – and admire the view!

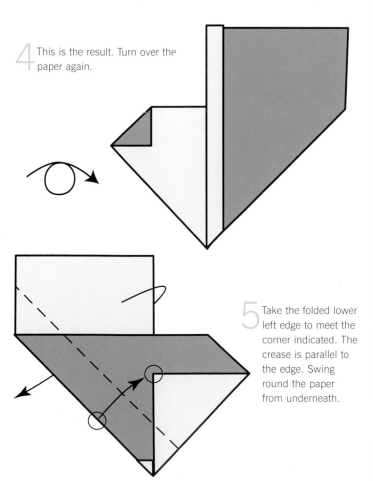

5 Take the folded lower left edge to meet the corner indicated. The crease is parallel to the edge. Swing round the paper from underneath.

CHALLENGE

The possibilities for this type of design are endless. Break things down into simple outlines, then use the two paper colours to form them. Try creating a design with a larger area of beach.

CD COVER

Traditional design

10 STEPS

This is a modern-day use of a very old Japanese design, known as a tato, or purse. Traditionally used to hold money or small presents, this model makes a practical container for a CD or DVD, which is inserted before you fold Step 7.

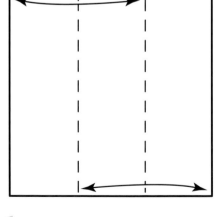

DIVIDING A SQUARE INTO THIRDS
REMINDER

Here's a third method for finding thirds. Compare it with the two methods on page 35.

1. Where the two diagonal creases meet marks a third.

2. Starting at the lower right corner, fold the lower left corner to touch the vertical halfway crease. Crease where shown and unfold.

3. Fold the lower right corner to touch the most recent crease. This is one third.

Paper size:
38 cm (15 in.) square
Finished CD cover:
12.5 cm (5 in.) square

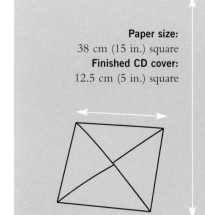

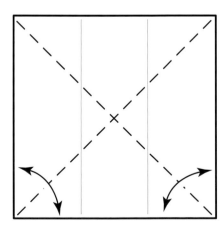

1 Start with a square, white side upwards. To hold a CD it should be 38 cm (15 in.) across. Divide one side into thirds (see reminder panel, above).

2 Add both diagonal creases.

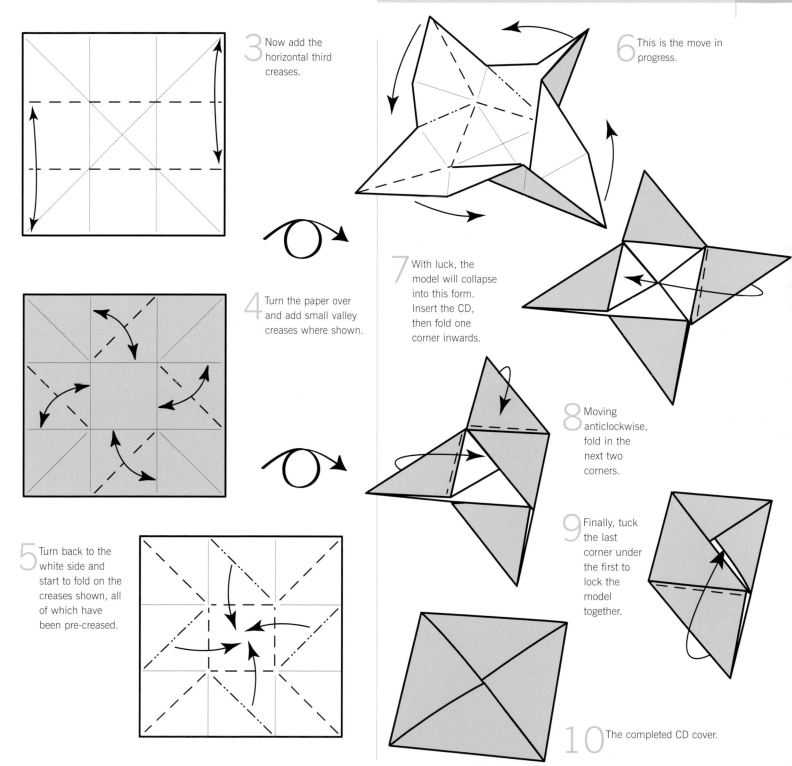

3 Now add the horizontal third creases.

4 Turn the paper over and add small valley creases where shown.

5 Turn back to the white side and start to fold on the creases shown, all of which have been pre-creased.

6 This is the move in progress.

7 With luck, the model will collapse into this form. Insert the CD, then fold one corner inwards.

8 Moving anticlockwise, fold in the next two corners.

9 Finally, tuck the last corner under the first to lock the model together.

10 The completed CD cover.

MASU BOX

Traditional design

10 STEPS

A masu box is a traditional Japanese wooden box, used for measuring rice, beans or, sometimes, sake. Many elegant wooden varieties can be bought. The paper version is also elegant, using simple, logical creases in a delightful folding sequence. The result is a perfect container that locks itself together and in many ways typifies traditional Japanese folding.

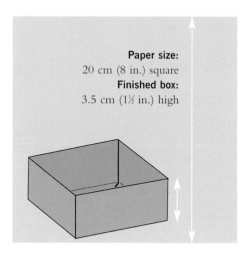

Paper size:
20 cm (8 in.) square
Finished box:
3.5 cm (1½ in.) high

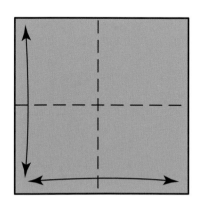

1 Start with a square, coloured side upwards. Fold in half both ways.

2 Turn over and fold the four corners to the centre (the technique of folding to the centre is known as a 'blintz').

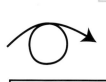

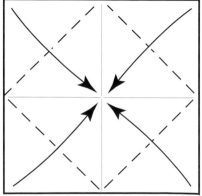

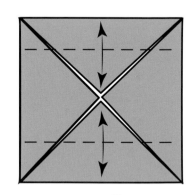

3 Fold two edges to the centre, crease and unfold.

4 Open out the upper and lower flaps.

5 Fold the sides to the centre, crease and unfold.

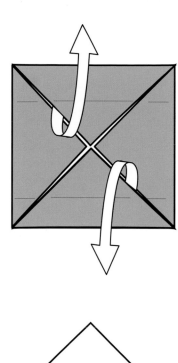

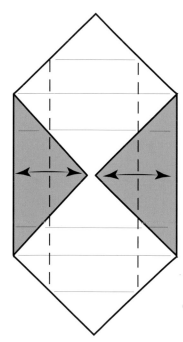

6 Following the creases carefully, refold the sides, raising the furthest corner towards you.

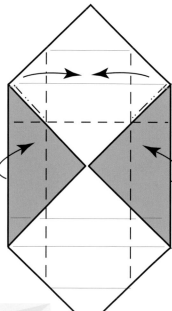

FOLDER'S TIP

Adjust the creases in Steps 3 and 5 to make a lid that fits perfectly.

7 Like this. Fold the flap into the centre of the box.

8 This should be the result. Rotate the paper.

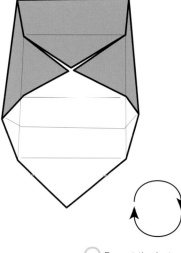

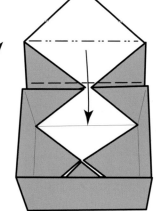

9 Repeat the last two steps.

10 The completed masu box.

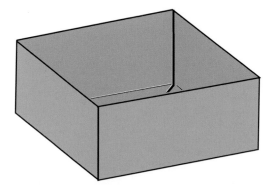

SQUARE DISSECTION PUZZLE

Design by Nick Robinson

10 STEPS

Many paper-folders are also interested in magic tricks, games and any kind of puzzle that requires a bit of thinking. One popular way of making a puzzle is to divide a shape into smaller identical sections and then challenge people to recreate it. These are known as dissection puzzles. Here is an origami version of a fairly well-known dissection. (Edwin Corrie of France has produced alternative methods of folding this shape.)

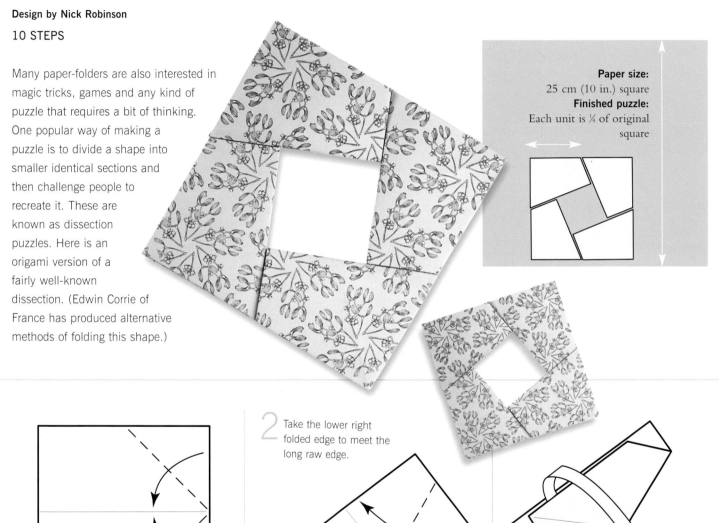

Paper size:
25 cm (10 in.) square
Finished puzzle:
Each unit is ¼ of original square

1 Start with a square, white side upwards, creased in half from top to bottom. Fold these two corners to meet the centre crease.

2 Take the lower right folded edge to meet the long raw edge.

3 Like this. Unfold the last step.

4 Unfold the right-hand coloured flap.

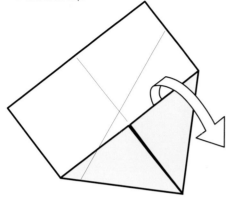

5 There are two locations to watch for here. Firstly, the corner will touch the halfway crease. Secondly, the long crease will lie upon itself. The circles show the reference points. Look at the next diagram carefully before making this fold.

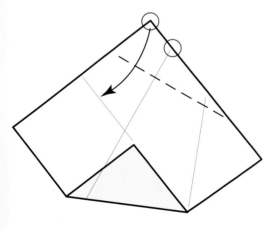

6 Refold the lower right corner on an existing crease.

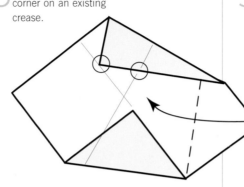

7 Again using an existing crease, fold over the lower section. Interlock the layers of paper to keep the flaps together.

interlock layers

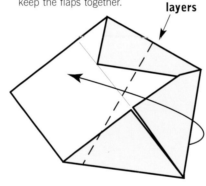

8 Fold over the narrow strip of white paper, tucking it underneath the upper flap. Interlock the layers at the end.

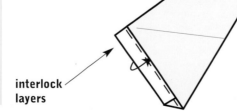

interlock layers

9 The unit is complete. You will need four units in total.

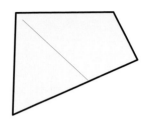

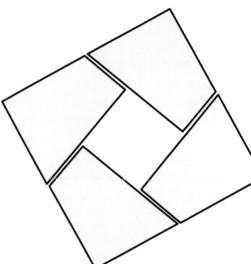

10 Here is one way of forming a square with the units, but there is also another method. You could even count the square hole in the middle as a third solution!

CHALLENGE

Can you find a new folding sequence for this shape, but one that gives a bigger finished shape when folded from the same sized starting square?

RECTANGULAR DISSECTION PUZZLE

Design by Nick Robinson

9 STEPS

The shapes of these dissection puzzles are fairly simple and not difficult to create with paper. The challenge is to achieve them using an efficient sequence of folds and to keep each unit neat and tidy, as well as locked together by overlapping papers. When you have run out of ideas starting with a square, you can then investigate the possibilities of a rectangle. The author created this design following a series of 'fold exchanges' with a fellow paper-folder David Mitchell, who has a keen interest in elegant geometric folding.

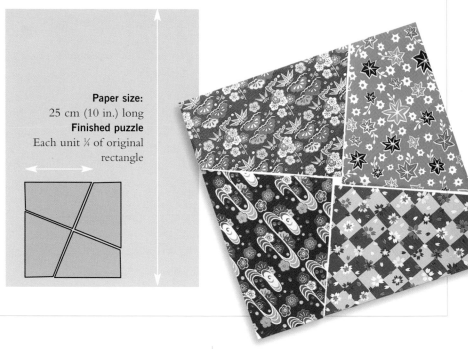

Paper size:
25 cm (10 in.) long
Finished puzzle
Each unit ¼ of original
rectangle

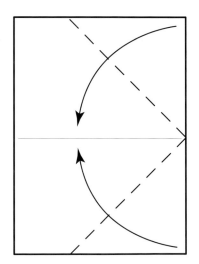

1 Start with a rectangle, creased in half. Fold each half of one side to the centre crease.

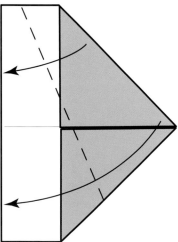

2 Take the upper folded edge to lie along the vertical raw edge.

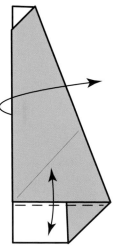

3 Crease along the lower folded edge, then unfold to Step 2.

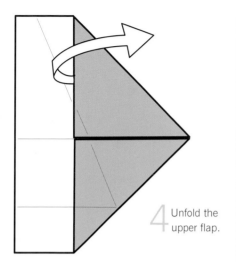

4 Unfold the upper flap.

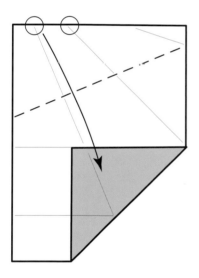

5 Note the circled reference points and check the next diagram to see where they will end up. Then fold the longest crease back down along its own length until the reference points meet.

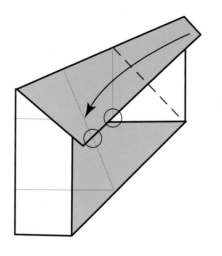

6 This should be the result. Fold a flap over on an existing crease.

interlock layers

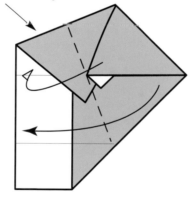

7 Again using an existing crease, fold the right half over. Interlock layers to hold the paper together.

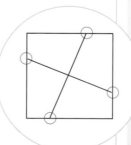

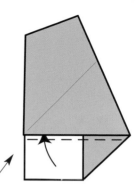

interlock layers

8 Tuck the lower flap inside, interlocking layers as you do so.

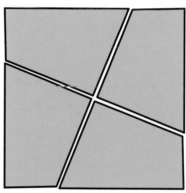

9 The unit is complete. This dissection puzzle works in the same way as the square-based version. Here is the alternative solution.

FOLDER'S TIP

Pasquale D'Auria of Italy had the bright idea of joining the units with string or rubber bands in the circled locations. The design turns inside out, alternating between one solution and the other. You can hide the bands within the paper.

GIRAFFE PASSING A WINDOW

Design by Nick Robinson

7 STEPS

Origami isn't noted for expressing humour through folds, but here's a rare exception. It's a paper version of a well-known visual joke. Quickly fold it and challenge your friends to figure out what it is. (By altering the size of the neck you can also create a brontosaurus passing a window!)

Paper size:
25 cm (10 in.) square
Finished model:
13 cm (5 in.) high

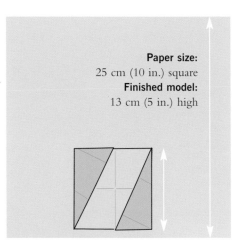

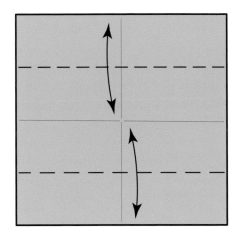

1 Start with a square, creased in half both ways. Add two quarter creases.

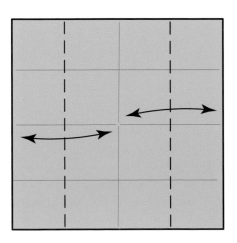

2 Add the other two quarter creases, then turn the paper over.

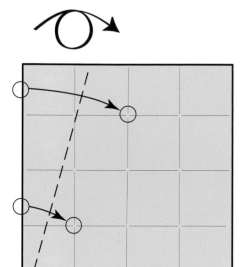

3 Fold so that the left-hand raw edge lies along the two reference points. These aren't critical, but help to get both sides of the neck parallel.

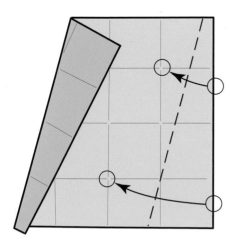

4 Repeat from the right-hand side.

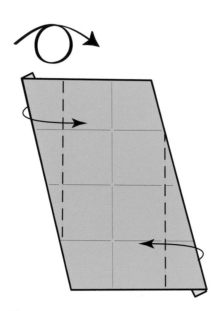

5 Turn the paper over. Fold inwards along the vertical quarter creases.

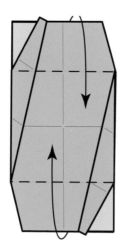

6 Repeat the folds on the horizontal quarter creases.

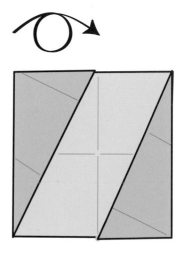

7 Turn over for the finished illusion.

CHALLENGE

Can you think of any similar visual jokes to translate into origami designs? How about a trombone in a telephone box? Please send them to the author if you can!

TEN-POINT STAR

Design by David Collier
10 STEPS

There seems to be no limit to the number of ways in which you can combine simple units into a ring to form stars or wreaths. Some folders from the Netherlands even use tea bags! However, you should still look for simplicity and elegance, amply demonstrated in this star by the late David Collier of England.

Paper size:
10 cm (4 in.) square
Finished star:
25 cm (10 in.) high

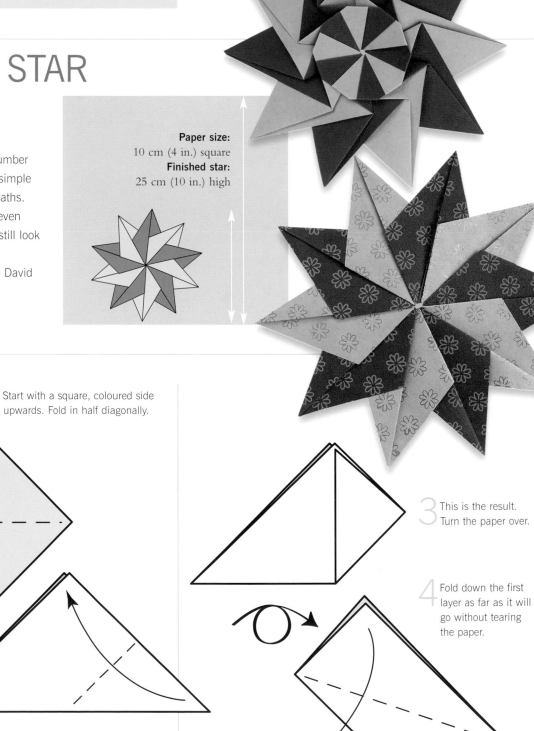

1 Start with a square, coloured side upwards. Fold in half diagonally.

2 Fold the lower right corner to meet the top corner.

3 This is the result. Turn the paper over.

4 Fold down the first layer as far as it will go without tearing the paper.

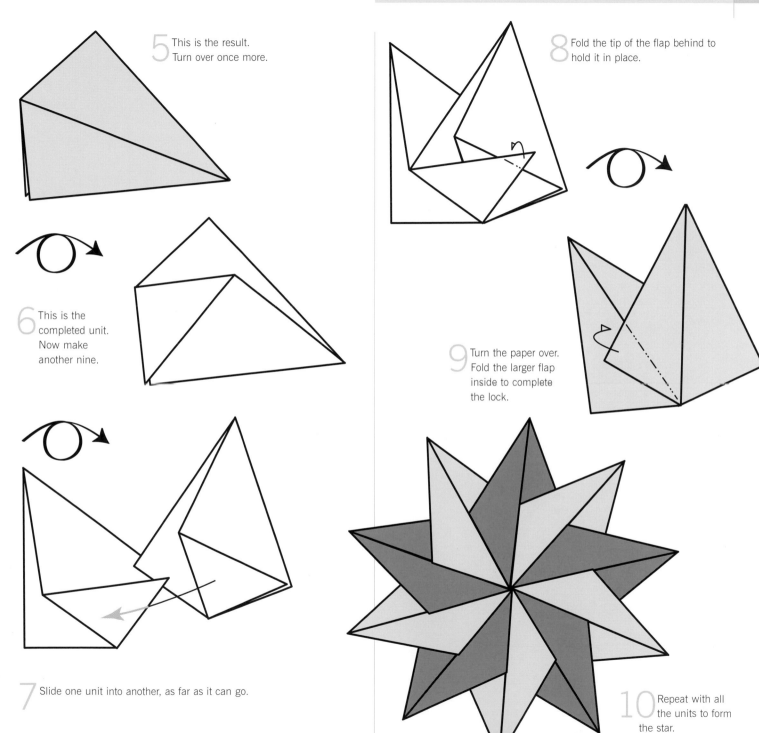

5 This is the result. Turn over once more.

6 This is the completed unit. Now make another nine.

7 Slide one unit into another, as far as it can go.

8 Fold the tip of the flap behind to hold it in place.

9 Turn the paper over. Fold the larger flap inside to complete the lock.

10 Repeat with all the units to form the star.

INTERMEDIATE PROJECTS

These designs focus on geometric subjects and other interesting designs, chosen to show the many different styles and subjects that are all part of origami. Often, looking at (for example) a cube, you might wonder where the fun is in folding such a basic shape. The answer is in the question – it is the folding that provides the enjoyment as much as looking at the finished object. The challenge is in folding neatly and producing perfect results.

MODULAR CUBE

Based on a unit by Mitsonobu Sonobe

12 STEPS

Although a basic shape, the cube holds endless fascination for creative paper-folders, who are always looking for new ways of designing one. Add to this the many possibilities for patterns on the face of a cube and you have the potential material for a lifetime's folding! As with any modular design (where several simple units are assembled to create a more complex whole), you need to fold accurately, or the result will not hold together well or look attractive.

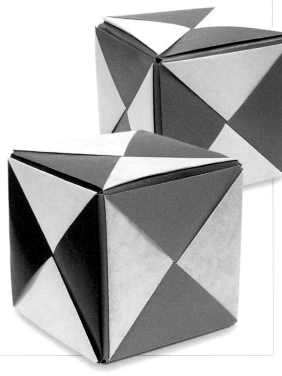

Paper size:
25 cm (10 in.) square
Finished cube:
13 cm (5 in.) wide

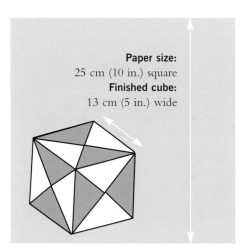

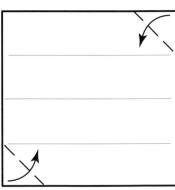

INSIDE REVERSE
REMINDER

1. Make a pre-crease.

2. Push the point inside.

3. Complete.

1 Start with a square, white side towards you, creased in half. Fold opposite sides to the centre, crease firmly and unfold.

2 Fold the opposite corners marked in the diagram to the quarter creases.

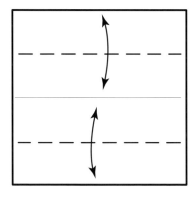

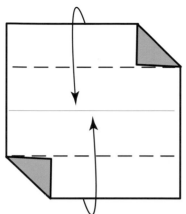

3 Refold along the quarter creases.

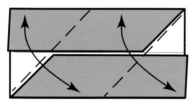

4 Pre-crease neatly where shown

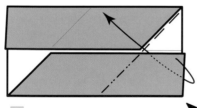

5 Inside-reverse fold the corner, (see reminder panel, left).

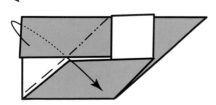

6 Repeat on the diagonally opposite corner.

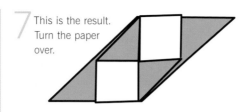

7 This is the result. Turn the paper over.

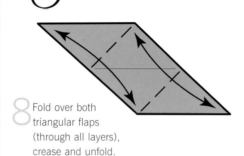

8 Fold over both triangular flaps (through all layers), crease and unfold.

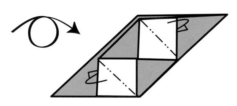

9 Turn over again, then tuck the outside white triangles into the pockets underneath.

10 This is the completed unit. Make six in total.

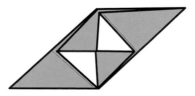

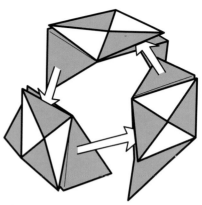

11 Assemble as shown. Make sure the coloured triangle tucks into the pocket formed by the white flap folded inside in Step 9. Assemble all six units loosely, then tighten.

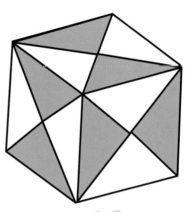

12 The completed cube.

CHALLENGE

There are many different polyhedra you can create with this unit. Try assembling eight, twelve and then thirty units. How about combining three to form a triangular pyramid unit?

TRIANGULAR BOX

Design by Nick Robinson

18 STEPS

This is an example of a design that may not be very exciting to look at, but contains a number of pleasing moves and techniques. Arguments rage in the origami world as to whether the sequence or the end result is the most important. With geometric designs, it's often the sequence – looking at the model isn't nearly as much fun as folding it! In this design, trouble has been taken to ensure that both the outside and the inside of the finished model are free from all creases. In order to achieve this, some creases don't extend as far as they could, which adds to the folding challenge. Try to fold neatly and accurately.

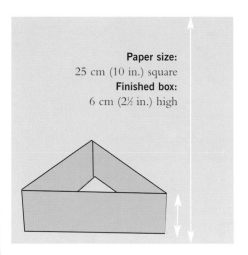

Paper size:
25 cm (10 in.) square
Finished box:
6 cm (2½ in.) high

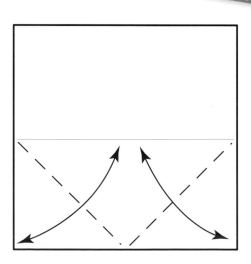

1 Start with a square, creased in half. Fold two corners to the centre crease, crease and unfold.

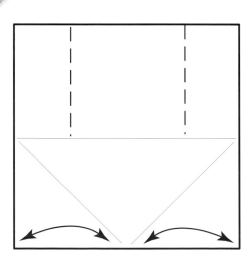

2 Mark the vertical quarter creases in the top half of the paper only.

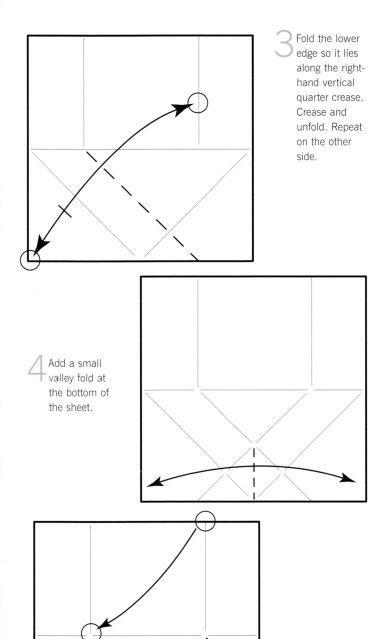

3 Fold the lower edge so it lies along the right-hand vertical quarter crease. Crease and unfold. Repeat on the other side.

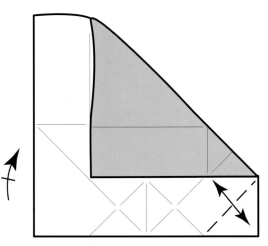

6 Fold the lower corner to meet the raw edge, crease and unfold.

4 Add a small valley fold at the bottom of the sheet.

7 Turn the paper over and use the location points to add two short creases.

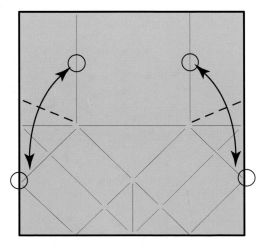

5 Fold so the indicated points meet. Only crease where shown.

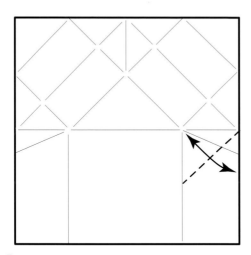

8 Turn back to the white side. Fold the right edge to the horizontal halfway crease, creasing only up to the quarter crease.

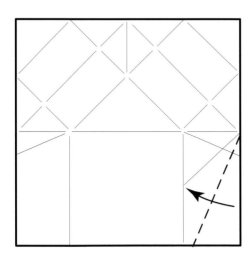

9 Fold the same side to the new crease.

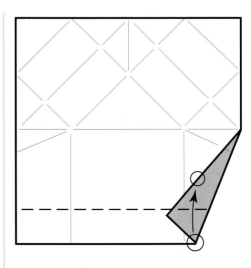

10 Take the lower right corner up to lie on the coloured edge. Use the quarter creases to ensure you are folding at right angles.

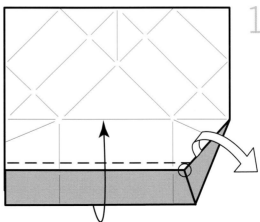

11 Pull out the paper folded over in Step 9. Fold the lower edge to lie exactly on the horizontal halfway crease.

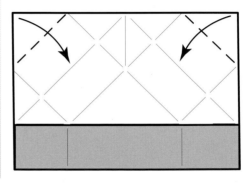

12 Fold in the upper corners.

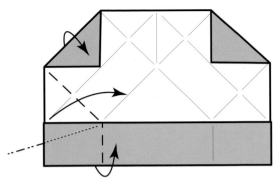

13 Use the creases shown to raise two sides and form a corner of the box. The dotted line indicates an existing mountain crease underneath. Check the next diagram for guidance.

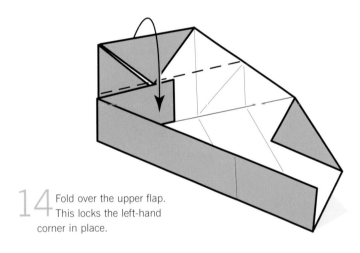

14 Fold over the upper flap. This locks the left-hand corner in place.

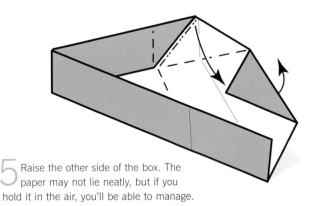

15 Raise the other side of the box. The paper may not lie neatly, but if you hold it in the air, you'll be able to manage.

16 Form the right-hand corner in the same way as in Step 12.

17 Tuck the flap inside.

18 The completed model.

CHALLENGE

Fold two similar boxes, then create a square box to put them in. Re-examine the folding sequence. Can you find another way of locating the crease in Step 11?

SKELETAL CUBE

Design by Jeff Beynon
8 STEPS

Simple folds can be joined together to form fascinating and apparently complex shapes. This design is a perfect example. Starting with the familiar fish base (see reminder panel, right), Jeff adds a few extra creases and builds a skeletal cube from twenty-four units. There are also many other ways in which you can combine different numbers of these units.

FISH BASE
REMINDER

1. Fold two sides to a diagonal.

2. Fold in half behind.

3. Pull down both corners.

4. Complete.

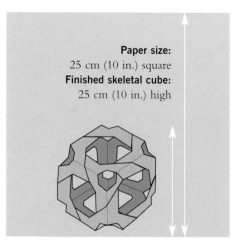

Paper size:
25 cm (10 in.) square
Finished skeletal cube:
25 cm (10 in.) high

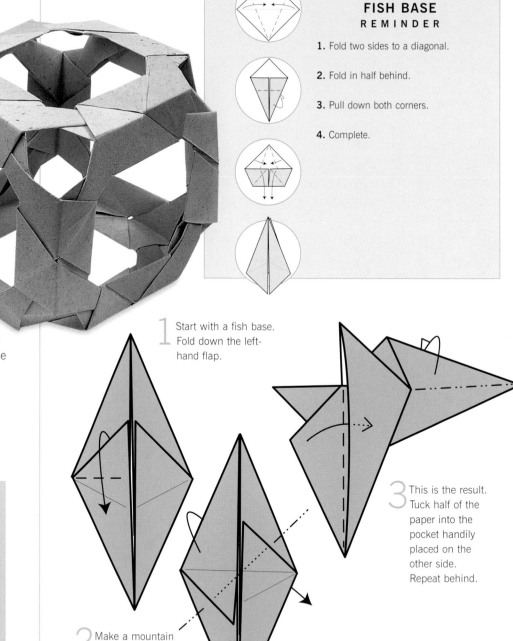

1 Start with a fish base. Fold down the left-hand flap.

2 Make a mountain fold at 45 degrees that passes through the centre of the paper.

3 This is the result. Tuck half of the paper into the pocket handily placed on the other side. Repeat behind.

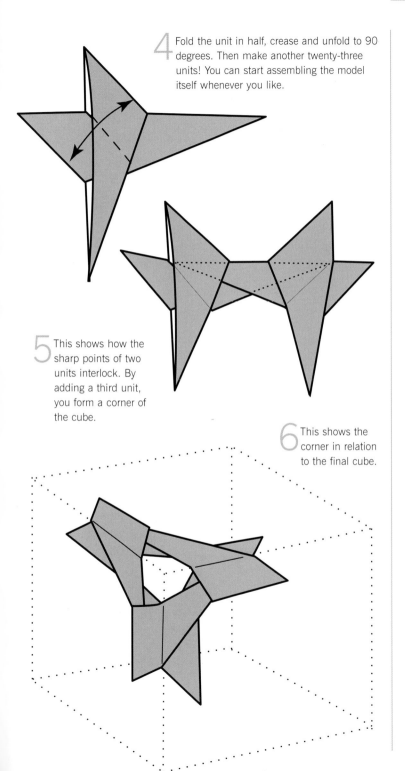

4 Fold the unit in half, crease and unfold to 90 degrees. Then make another twenty-three units! You can start assembling the model itself whenever you like.

5 This shows how the sharp points of two units interlock. By adding a third unit, you form a corner of the cube.

6 This shows the corner in relation to the final cube.

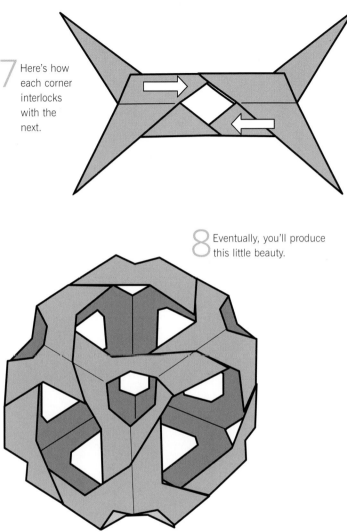

7 Here's how each corner interlocks with the next.

8 Eventually, you'll produce this little beauty.

CHALLENGE
Can you form any other polyhedra apart from a cube? For example, by joining two or four units and combining them with three units.

ALI'S DISH

Design by Nick Robinson

8 STEPS

For many years the author has had a passion for creating origami dishes, inspired by the superb work of origami master Philip Shen. The aim is to create designs that are elegant, efficient and accurately creased, and that hold together with minimal use of origami techniques. The best designs often seem simply to emerge from a set of familiar creases, as if they had been lying there waiting to be discovered.

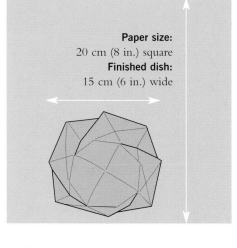

Paper size:
20 cm (8 in.) square
Finished dish:
15 cm (6 in.) wide

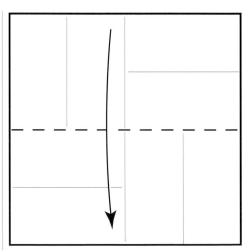

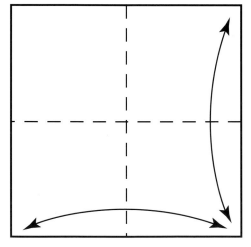
1 Start with a square, white side upwards. Crease from side to opposite side both ways.

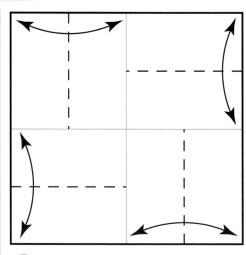
2 Add quarter creases that only extend as far as the centre crease.

3 Fold in half from top to bottom.

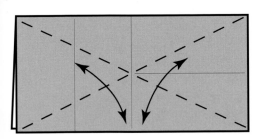

4 Add both diagonals in the 2 x 1 rectangle. Repeat on the other side, then open out, fold in half the other way and repeat on both sides.

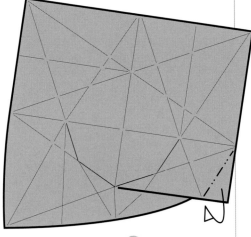

6 Fold the flap behind on an existing crease.

8 Gently press in the centre from underneath, encouraging the dish to become slightly rounded.

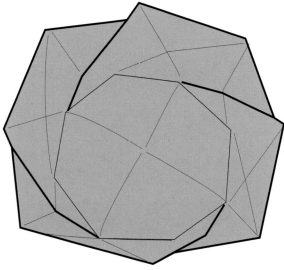

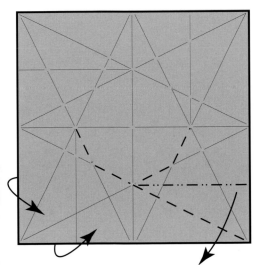

5 Open back out to the coloured side. Form the paper into three dimensions, concentrating on the mountain crease. The centre of the paper forms the centre of the dish, so the sides should come up slightly.

7 Here is the same fold seen from the side. Tuck it behind the layer of paper. Repeat on the three remaining sides.

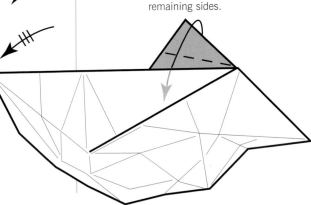

CHALLENGE

Look at the final dish – several of the creases are not used. Mark them with a pen, then unfold and try to create the same dish without these creases. It will mean some creases are only partially complete.

MONEY BOX

Design by Christoph Mangutsch

11 STEPS

This is an adaptation of the classic waterbomb model. By extending the apparent width of the square, you move the locking mechanisms further apart, leaving a storage space in the centre. It's a great example of how existing folds can be adapted to produce new ones, with just a little thought and experimentation.

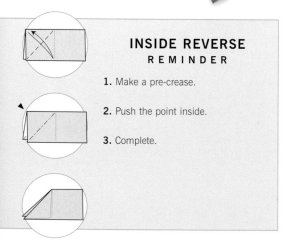

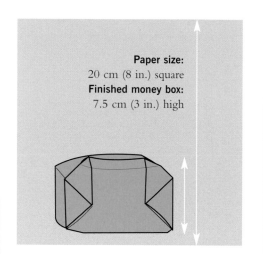

Paper size:
20 cm (8 in.) square
Finished money box:
7.5 cm (3 in.) high

INSIDE REVERSE
REMINDER

1. Make a pre-crease.

2. Push the point inside.

3. Complete.

1 Start with a square, white side upwards. Crease in half from bottom to top.

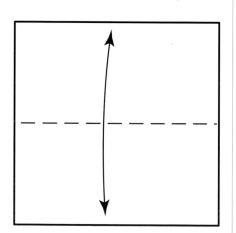

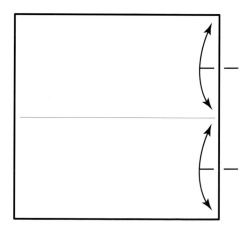

2 Add pinches to mark the quarter distances.

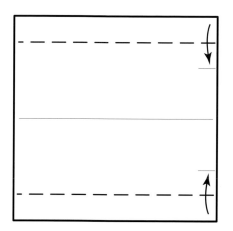

3 Fold the top and bottom edges to the pinch marks.

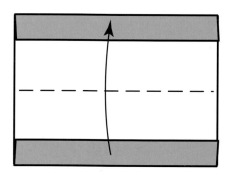

4 Fold in half again.

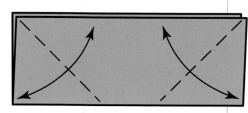

5 Fold the shorter edges to the top edge, crease and unfold.

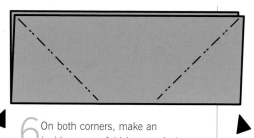

6 On both corners, make an inside-reverse fold (see reminder panel, left).

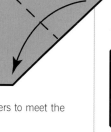

7 Fold all outer corners to meet the lower corners.

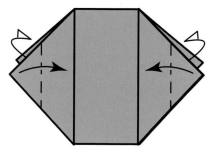

8 Fold the new outer corners to the centre of the inside folded edges, on each side.

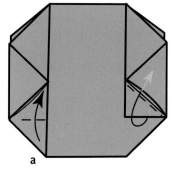

9 Fold the lower triangle in half (a). Tuck the small triangle into the pocket (b).

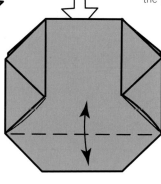

10 Fold over the lower corner, crease and unfold. Then blow hard inside the gap at the top to inflate the box. Finally, pinch it into shape.

11 The completed money box.

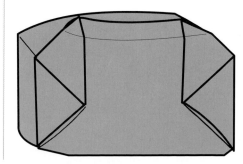

DOUBLE FISH TESSELLATION

Design by Nick Robinson
12 STEPS

Tessellations are shapes laid next to each other to form a tiled effect. This double fish uses techniques similar to those of a cube unit, but is begun from a rectangular sheet of paper. Interestingly, you can use any shape of rectangle to fold this design.

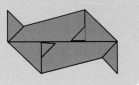

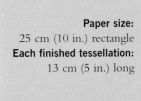

Paper size:
25 cm (10 in.) rectangle
Each finished tessellation:
13 cm (5 in.) long

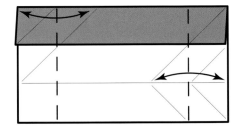

1 Start with a rectangle, creased in half widthways. Fold the long edges to the centre crease.

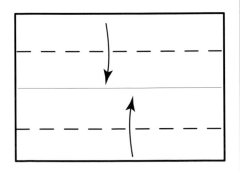

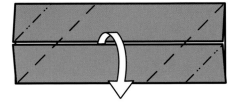

2 Fold the short sides to the long sides, then fold the corners back again before unfolding. Unfold the lower edge.

3 Using the location points shown, fold in the short edges, crease and unfold.

4 Inside-reverse the top-left corner.

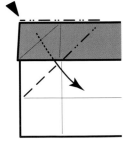

5 Form the tail fin by making an inside-reverse fold.

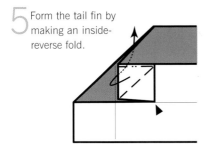

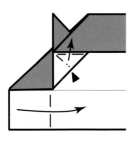

6 Swivel the small triangle in half upwards as you fold the left-hand side across. Check the next diagram for guidance.

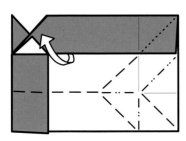

7 Carefully pull the layer out from underneath, tucking the triangle inside. Repeat Steps 4 to 6 on the right-hand side.

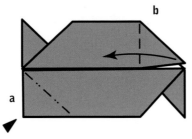

8 Pre-crease and inside reverse the corner point (a). Fold the flap over (b).

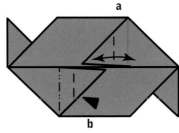

9 Pre-crease (a), then make an inside-reverse fold on the point (b).

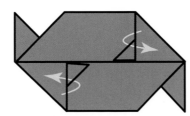

10 Open up the nose section of the fish slightly. Underneath the inside-reverse fold you have just made, there is a layer of paper. Pull this out and carefully tuck the reversed flap underneath it. Re-form the nose. Repeat on the other nose.

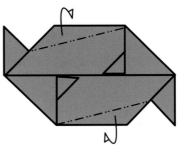

11 Shape the backs of both fish to complete the tessellation.

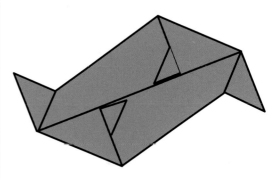

12 The finished tessellation.

CHALLENGE

A similar 'double' fish can be made from a square, but it becomes squat and less fishlike. Can you alter the folding sequence to make a narrow fish from a square?

ALSO SEE

Reverse folding **page 18**
Modular cube **page 68**

BABY EAGLE

Design by Lore Schirokauer
17 STEPS

When creating a bird, many folders naturally start with a bird base, as it has clear points for creating wings, heads or legs. You can, however, use other bases as starting points or – as with this design – a combination of bases. This fold starts with a preliminary base, one side of which is folded into half of a bird base. The other side (with a slight modification) becomes half of a frog base. This combination allows you to position the flaps and points in different places to the standard bird base.

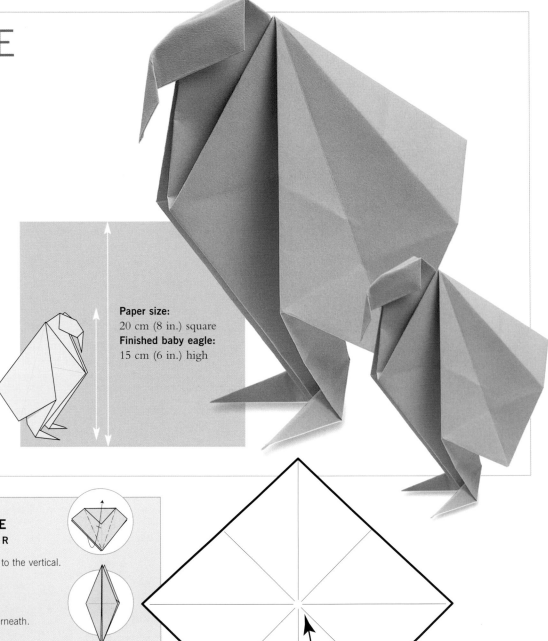

Paper size:
20 cm (8 in.) square
Finished baby eagle:
15 cm (6 in.) high

BIRD BASE
REMINDER

1. Preliminary base, fold sides to the vertical.

2. Fold the top section down.

3. Pull out the flaps from underneath.

4. Lift the lower corner carefully. Repeat behind.

5. Complete.

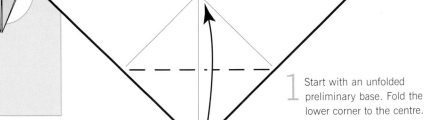

1 Start with an unfolded preliminary base. Fold the lower corner to the centre.

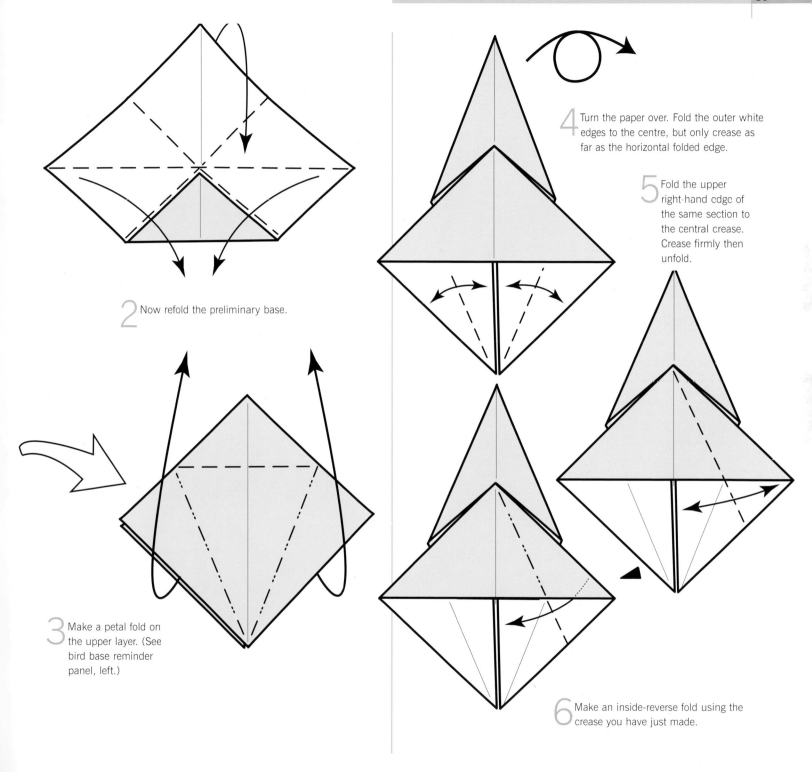

2 Now refold the preliminary base.

3 Make a petal fold on the upper layer. (See bird base reminder panel, left.)

4 Turn the paper over. Fold the outer white edges to the centre, but only crease as far as the horizontal folded edge.

5 Fold the upper right-hand edge of the same section to the central crease. Crease firmly then unfold.

6 Make an inside-reverse fold using the crease you have just made.

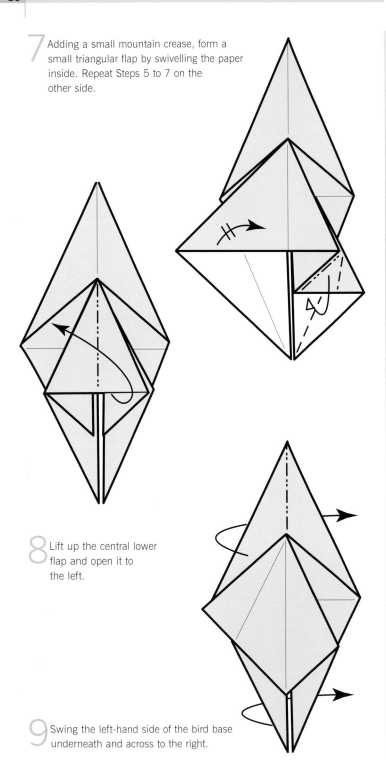

7 Adding a small mountain crease, form a small triangular flap by swivelling the paper inside. Repeat Steps 5 to 7 on the other side.

8 Lift up the central lower flap and open it to the left.

9 Swing the left-hand side of the bird base underneath and across to the right.

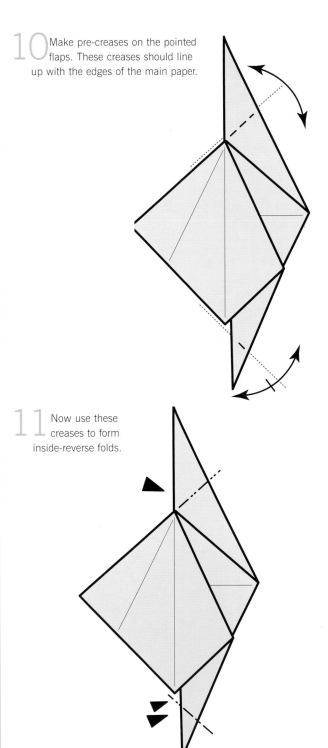

10 Make pre-creases on the pointed flaps. These creases should line up with the edges of the main paper.

11 Now use these creases to form inside-reverse folds.

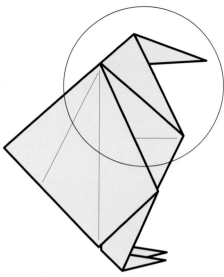

12 Most of the bird is now complete, but you need to refine the head.

13 Pre-crease and make an outside-reverse fold on the head. The paper at the top of the head forms a small pocket.

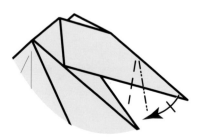

14 Crimp the end of the beak.

FOLDER'S TIP

You may need to adjust the angle of the feet slightly if the bird isn't stable. The creases forming the head can be altered to create other types of bird, such as a chicken.

15 The head is now complete.

ALSO SEE

Reverse folding **page 18**
Crimp **page 22**
Petal **page 23**
Preliminary base **page 28**

16 Open the sides of the wings slightly, flattening a triangular section at the back. This makes the bird three-dimensional and more lifelike.

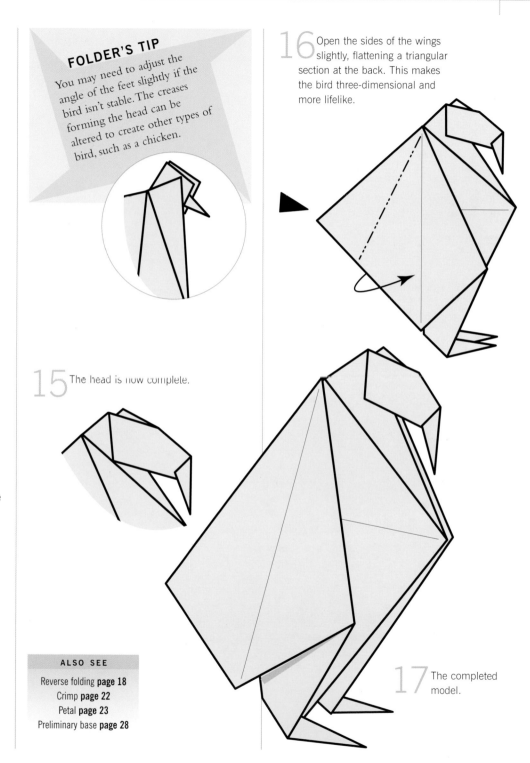

17 The completed model.

SQUARE BEAR

Design by Edwin Corrie

19 STEPS

The work of a truly creative origami designer has a distinct character. In other words, you can often recognize the designer from the design. Edwin Corrie is such a folder. His models can easily be picked out because they reflect the particular techniques and styles that he enjoys using. While some creators strive for realism, Corrie simplifies the form of the subject and produces a clearly recognizable caricature. Another feature of his work is his development of an efficient folding sequence that produces the same model every time – there is no need to guess angles or distances.

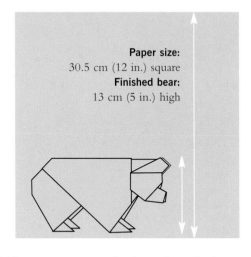

Paper size:
30.5 cm (12 in.) square
Finished bear:
13 cm (5 in.) high

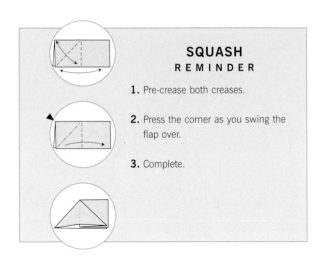

SQUASH
REMINDER

1. Pre-crease both creases.

2. Press the corner as you swing the flap over.

3. Complete.

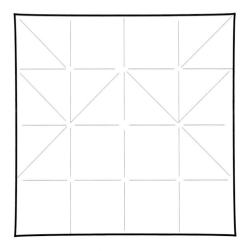

1 Start with a square, divided into quarters both ways. Add the creases shown.

2 Form a rabbit's ear, swinging the flap to the right.

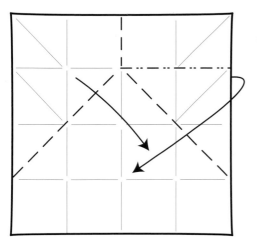

5 Fold up the matching corner.

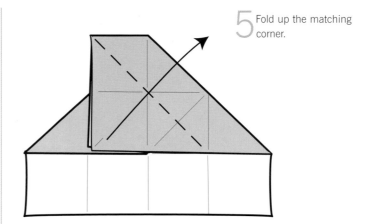

3 Fold over the upper corner.

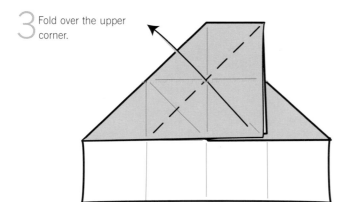

6 Here is a swivel fold. To make the move successfully you need to fold all the creases together. Fold and unfold until you understand how it works.

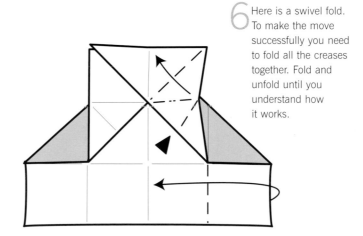

4 Swing the central section to the left.

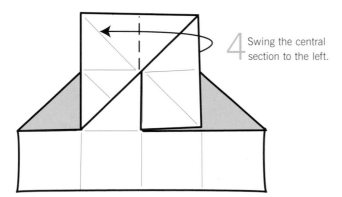

7 Swing the small triangle to the right.

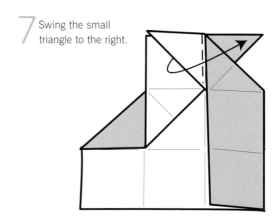

8 Make another swivel fold similar to the one made in Step 6.

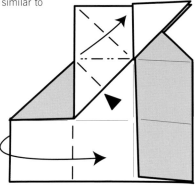

9 Squash the central point (see reminder panel, page 88).

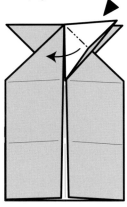

10 Tuck the sides of the squashed flap under the layers on either side.

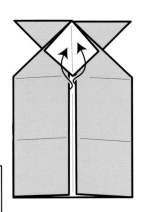

11 Fold the lower edge to the top of the paper.

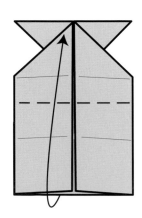

12 Turn over the paper. Fold up the lower flap between the bottom corners of the triangular section. Allow the paper to swing round from underneath.

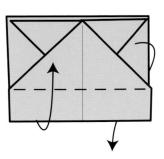

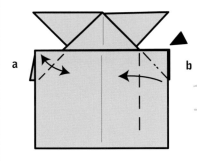

a

b

13 Fold over the corners, crease and unfold (a). Fold in the side, squash-folding at the top (b).

14 Fold the model in half from right to left.

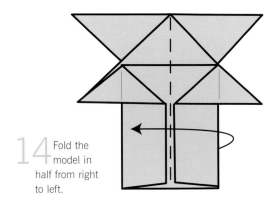

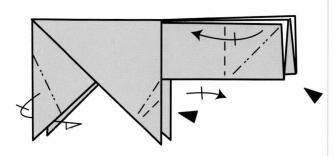

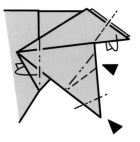

15 Rotate the paper to this position. Several steps are shown in this diagram. Mountain-fold the rear legs. Inside-crimp the front legs. Squash to create the ears. Then repeat all these steps on the other side.

18 Various shaping folds are made to finish the head (follow the diagram).

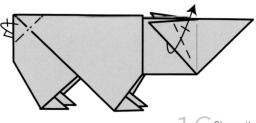

16 Shape the rump and fold the ears up.

19 The completed bear.

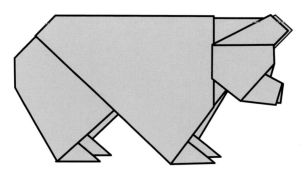

17 Make an outside crimp to form the head.

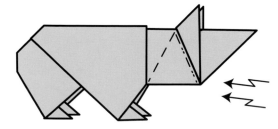

FOLDER'S TIP

This fold really requires thin paper because the extra layers in the back cause problems. Paper does have width and you need to take account of it.

ALSO SEE
Crimp **page 22**

STAR UNIT

Design by Nick Robinson

7 STEPS

Unlike the ten-point star, this design is three-dimensional and therefore perfect for making decorations. You need at least five star units to make a finished design in three dimensions, but the number of extra units you may use is limited only by the thickness of the paper and your patience. This design was also independently created by Tomoko Fuse of Japan. With such simple designs, duplication is likely to happen. Fortunately, most people in the origami world are happy to share credit when they learn that another folder has been thinking along similar lines.

KITE BASE
REMINDER

1. Fold one side to a diagonal.

2. Repeat on the other side.

3. Complete.

ALSO SEE

Reverse folding **page 18**
Ten-point star **page 64**

Paper size:
15 cm (6 in.) square
Finished star:
15 cm (6 in.) high

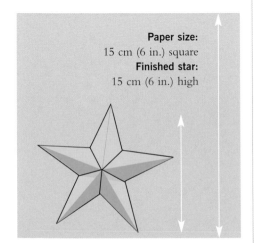

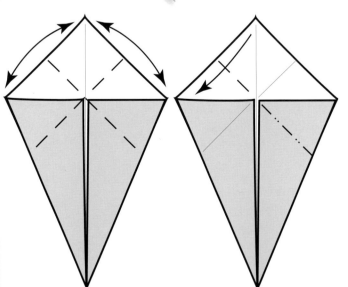

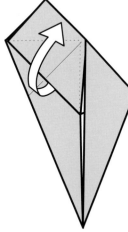

1 Start with a kite base (see reminder panel, above). Fold the top corner to each of the outer corners, crease and unfold.

2 Fold the top corner to the left-hand corner, inside-reverse fold on the right.

3 Pull out the layer of paper from underneath.

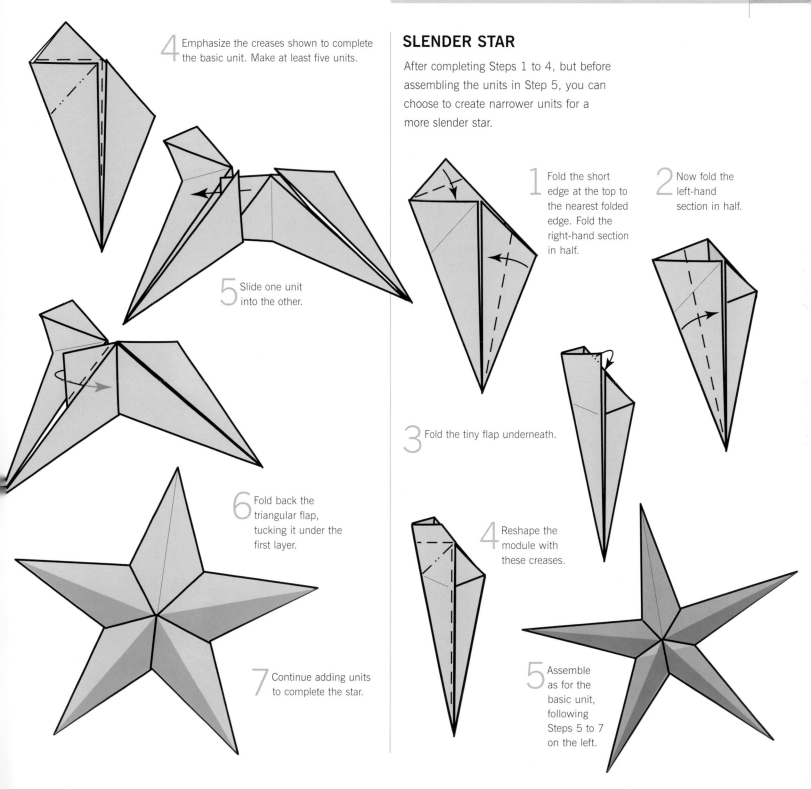

4 Emphasize the creases shown to complete the basic unit. Make at least five units.

5 Slide one unit into the other.

6 Fold back the triangular flap, tucking it under the first layer.

7 Continue adding units to complete the star.

SLENDER STAR

After completing Steps 1 to 4, but before assembling the units in Step 5, you can choose to create narrower units for a more slender star.

1 Fold the short edge at the top to the nearest folded edge. Fold the right-hand section in half.

2 Now fold the left-hand section in half.

3 Fold the tiny flap underneath.

4 Reshape the module with these creases.

5 Assemble as for the basic unit, following Steps 5 to 7 on the left.

PEACOCK

Design by Edwin Corrie

14 STEPS

This is another example of Corrie's work. To the front of a fairly well-known peacock (the head and legs are taken from a rectangle-based peacock by Adolfo Cerceda) he adds a radically new and elegant tail. You may find it interesting to compare this design with his square bear (page 88) and see if you can find any stylistic similarities.

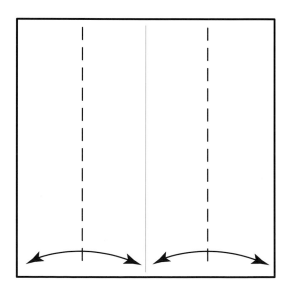

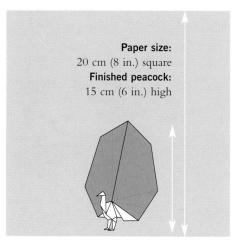

Paper size:
20 cm (8 in.) square
Finished peacock:
15 cm (6 in.) high

1 Start with a square, white side upwards, that has been creased in half. Add two quarter creases.

DOUBLE RABBIT'S EAR
REMINDER

1. Make an inside-reverse fold.

2. Pre-crease in half.

3. Another inside-reverse fold, repeat behind.

4. Complete.

2 Add valley creases where shown.

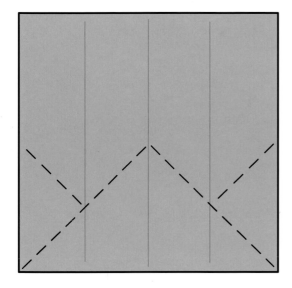

3 Follow the crease pattern carefully to produce a series of reverse folds. Check the next diagram as a guide.

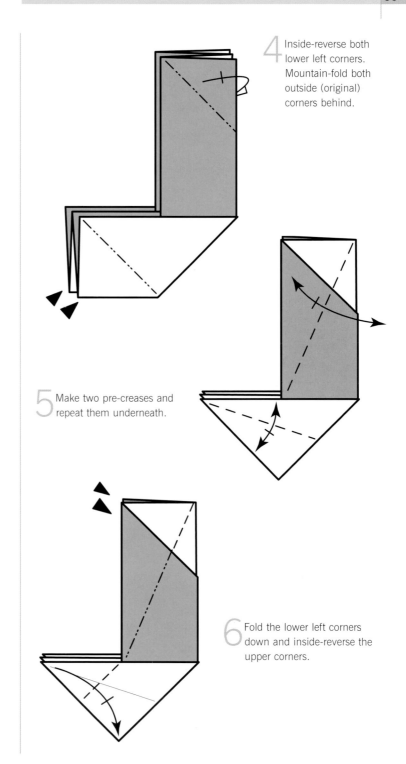

4 Inside-reverse both lower left corners. Mountain-fold both outside (original) corners behind.

5 Make two pre-creases and repeat them underneath.

6 Fold the lower left corners down and inside-reverse the upper corners.

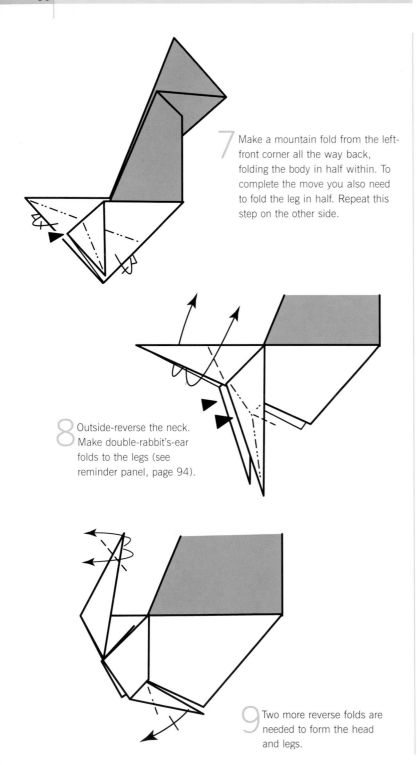

7 Make a mountain fold from the left-front corner all the way back, folding the body in half within. To complete the move you also need to fold the leg in half. Repeat this step on the other side.

8 Outside-reverse the neck. Make double-rabbit's-ear folds to the legs (see reminder panel, page 94).

9 Two more reverse folds are needed to form the head and legs.

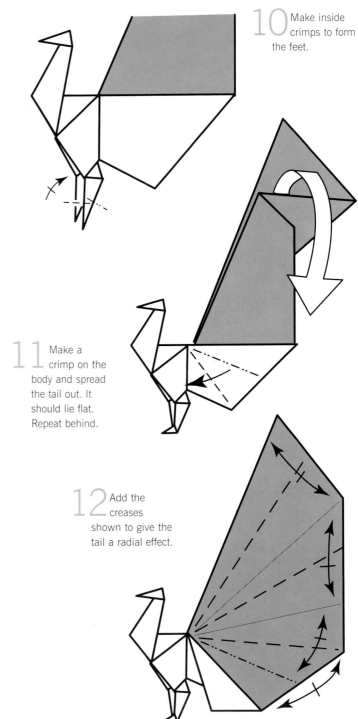

10 Make inside crimps to form the feet.

11 Make a crimp on the body and spread the tail out. It should lie flat. Repeat behind.

12 Add the creases shown to give the tail a radial effect.

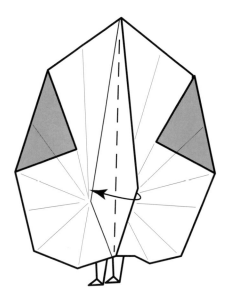

13 From behind the tail, make a valley fold to lock the tail together.

14 With a bit of balancing, you might even get your peacock to stand!

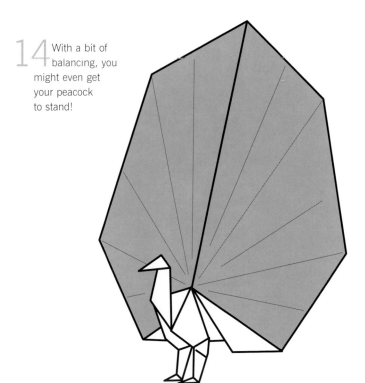

CHALLENGE
Find two sheets of thin paper, one a suitable body colour, the other a bright tail pattern. Glue the two sheets together with spray-mount adhesive and fold the perfect peacock!

ALSO SEE
Reverse folding **page 18**
Crimp **page 22**

SPINNING SYMMETRY

Design by Brian Cole

12 STEPS

This design is an exercise in accurate folding and produces a neat octagonal result. Cole, although an accomplished folder, was not usually creative. He was just playing about with creases when he stumbled upon this design. Sometimes, creativity needs only a flash of insight.

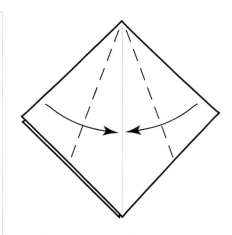

Paper size:
20 cm (8 in.) square
Finished model:
10 cm (4 in.) wide

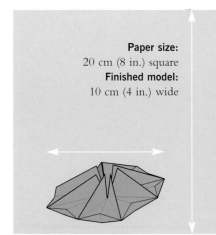

1 Start with a preliminary base, white side outwards. Fold both upper edges to the vertical crease.

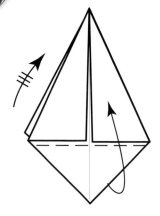

2 Fold the lower triangular flap upwards. Repeat in the other three possible places.

3 Open out back to the square.

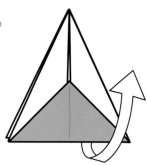

4 Fold the corners in on existing creases.

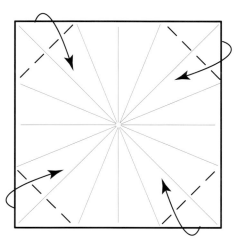

5 Fold an edge to the centre, creasing only where shown. Repeat on all eight sides. Turn the paper over.

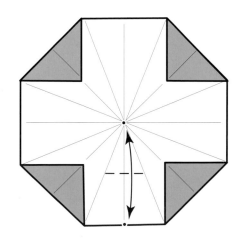

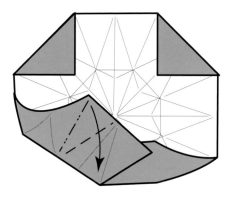

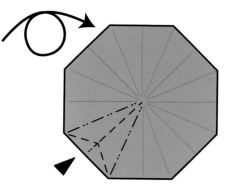

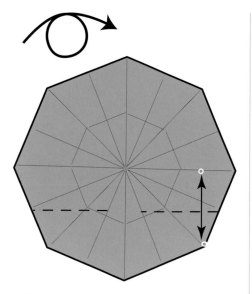

6 Fold the lower right corner to the horizontal crease, creasing only where shown. Repeat on all eight sides.

8 Here is one corner complete. Rotate the paper anticlockwise, repeating the move on all eight sides.

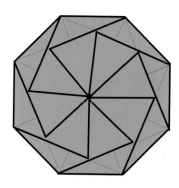

9 The last fold requires you to open the first one slightly. This will be the result.

10 Turn over the paper and reinforce these creases. From this side, the centre of the paper is the high point of a gentle cone shape.

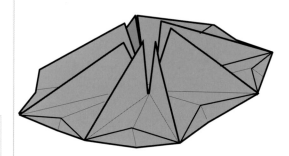

11 Turn over again. The paper should resemble an old-fashioned spinning top, with flaps that rotate anticlockwise, overlapping each other. This is a side view.

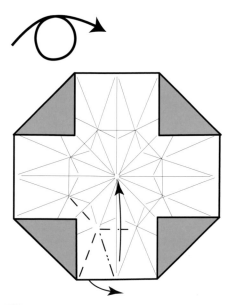

7 Turn over again and form a kind of rabbit's ear. As you do so, the paper will become three-dimensional.

CHALLENGE

Just for fun, make a mirror image of this design, folding the paper clockwise at Step 7. Also try making a tiny model and spinning it in the palm of your hand.

12 The completed model.

ALSO SEE
Rabbit's ear **page 20**
Preliminary base **page 28**

JET PLANE

Design by Nick Robinson

11 STEPS

Here is a simple jet plane, of the non-flying variety. Due to the way in which paper planes are built (with the majority of the paper at the front end), it isn't possible to make a flying plane with this wing shape.

Paper size:
15 cm (6 in.) square
Finished jet plane:
15 cm (6 in.) long

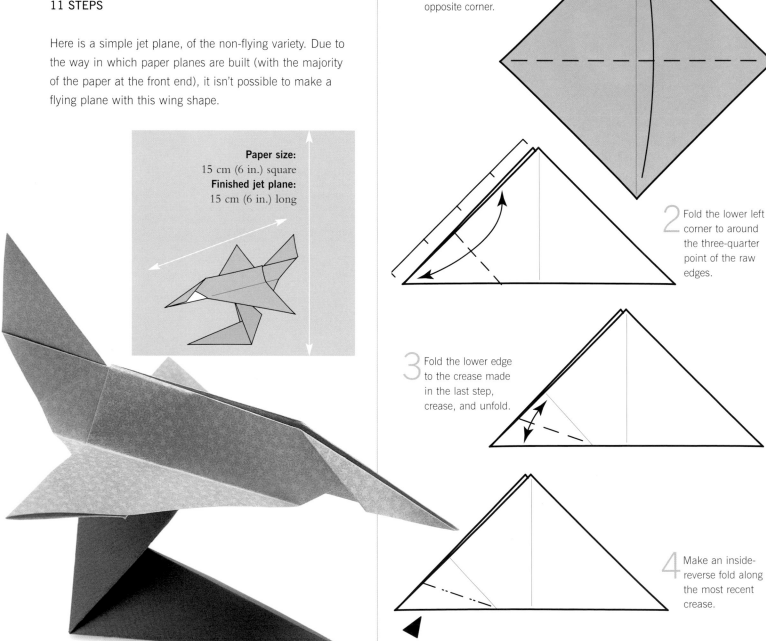

1 Start with a square of paper, coloured side upwards, with a diagonal crease. Fold in half from corner to opposite corner.

2 Fold the lower left corner to around the three-quarter point of the raw edges.

3 Fold the lower edge to the crease made in the last step, crease, and unfold.

4 Make an inside-reverse fold along the most recent crease.

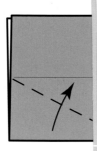

3 Carefully form [...] the left and lo[...] two creases.

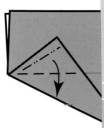

4 Fold the upper [...] the horizontal h[...] back the tiny se[...]

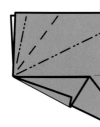

5 Here is the resu[...] two steps on the[...] then unfold bac[...]

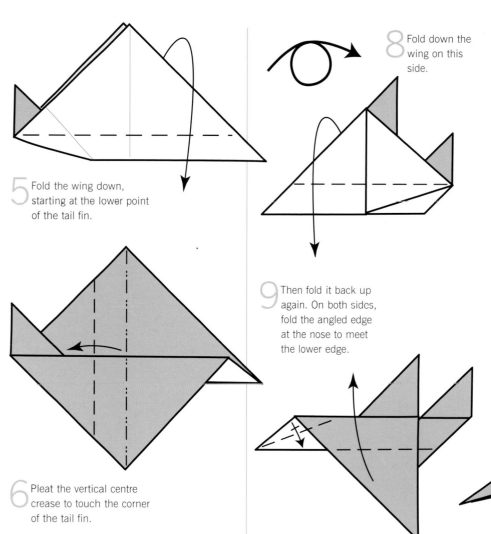

5 Fold the wing down, starting at the lower point of the tail fin.

6 Pleat the vertical centre crease to touch the corner of the tail fin.

7 Fold the wing upwards and turn over the paper.

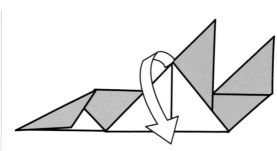

8 Fold down the wing on this side.

9 Then fold it back up again. On both sides, fold the angled edge at the nose to meet the lower edge.

CHALLENGE

Can you create the stand shown by adding a few creases to a fish base? You need to persuade the fish base to become three-dimensional, then make a reverse fold.

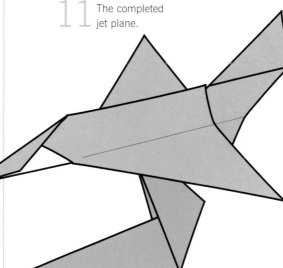

10 Fold both wings down to halfway.

11 The completed jet plane.

ALSO SEE
Fish base **page 30**
Inside reverse **page 18**

DOU...

Design by D...

17 STEPS

The design...
origami illu...
skilled artis...
him to visu...
unusual pe...
create them...
design was...
became a s...
cube appea...
through the...
You should...
colours or...
the effect.

TWISTED PAPER

Concept by Shuzo Fujimoto

9 AND 7 STEPS

Some origami techniques don't appear to have a clear place within conventional designs, but are nonetheless fascinating and often highly decorative in their own right. This technique allows you to take a square within the paper and rotate it through 90 degrees. In order to do this, a vertical strip of paper that is the width of half of the diagonal of that square is lost underneath the sheet. The same amount is lost horizontally, so you can see that the initial square quickly becomes much smaller. In order to learn this technique, try creating a single twist, then applying it on a smaller scale to a larger sheet of paper, creating nine twists. This will require a lot of patience on your part, but will ultimately make you a better folder.

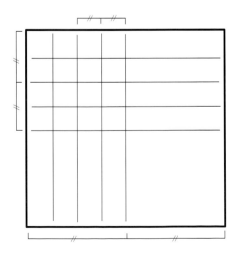

Paper size:
20 cm (8 in.) square
Finished model:
15 cm (6 in.) square

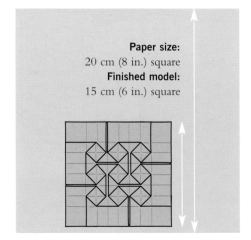

SINGLE TWIST

1 Start with a square and add the halfway creases, followed by the quarter and eighth creases in one quarter of the square.

2 Form a square using valley folds at 45 degrees to the existing creases.

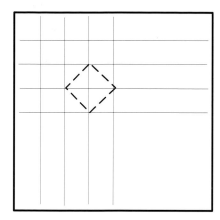

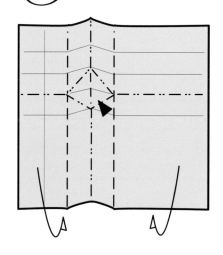

3 Turn the paper over. Fold some of the paper underneath, pressing in the vertical crease at the centre of the small square.

4 This is the result. Fold the upper section to the left and fold the matching section underneath to the right.

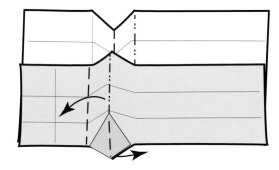

5 Fold down using the quarter crease.

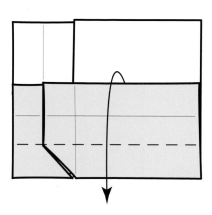

6 This is the result. Turn the paper over.

7 Fold down the three-eighths section.

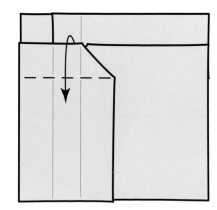

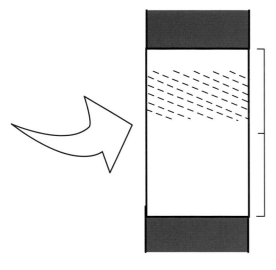

7 The view gets larger here and the outer sections are hidden for clarity. Add slanted creases at 45 degrees to the sides. This simulates the screw at the top of the tube.

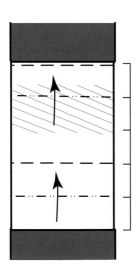

8 Make two pleats as shown. Each pleat is about one-fifth of the height of the white paper.

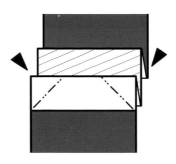

9 Inside-reverse fold the white corners.

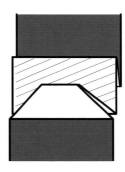

10 Like so. Turn the paper over.

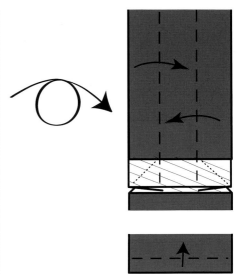

11 Fold the lower edge in slightly. Fold the sides of the upper section over each other and slide one inside the other to 'lock' together.

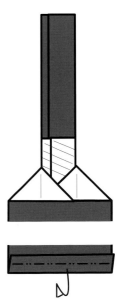

12 Fold half of the double layer at the bottom behind.

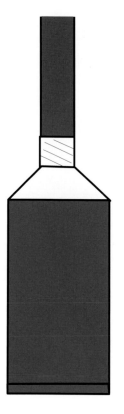

13 Turn the paper over. This is the basic tube. Now we concentrate on the paint itself.

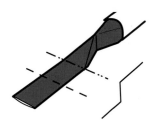

16 Make a right-angled corner.

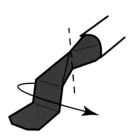

18 Swing the paper to the right using the crease pinched in Step 15.

14 Make the paint into a tube and pinch near the cap.

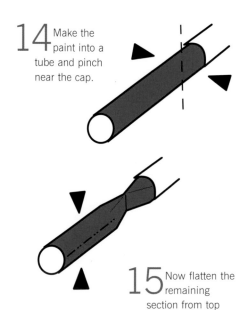

15 Now flatten the remaining section from top to bottom.

17 Fold the tips underneath.

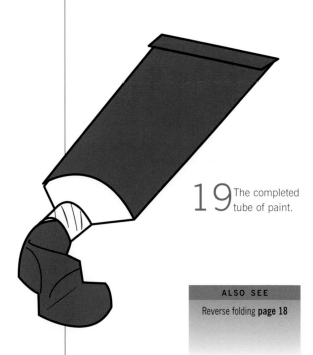

19 The completed tube of paint.

ALSO SEE

Reverse folding page 18

FLORAL POT

Design by Jeff Beynon

7 STEPS

The aim in creating origami pots or containers is to keep them simple and elegant, but make sure that they hold their form. While the creasing for this design may seem quite complicated, it is in essence a very simple model. The creases you need are all shown in Step 5. The preceding steps are used to create and locate these creases precisely.

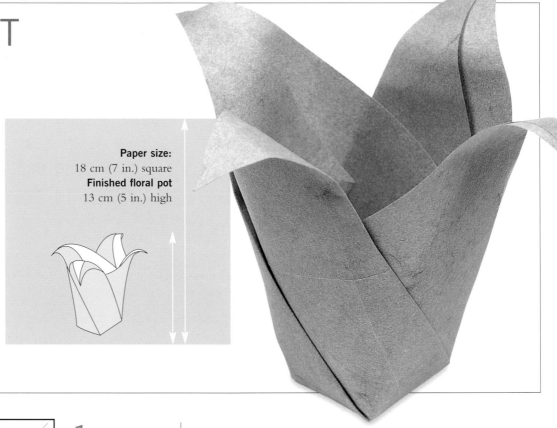

Paper size:
18 cm (7 in.) square
Finished floral pot
13 cm (5 in.) high

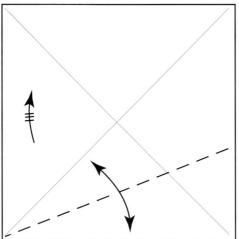

1 Start with a square, white side upwards, with both diagonals creased. Fold one side to the diagonal, crease and unfold. Repeat the same fold on each side.

2 The previous creases have formed the reference points for another four folds. Make sure you crease carefully and accurately.

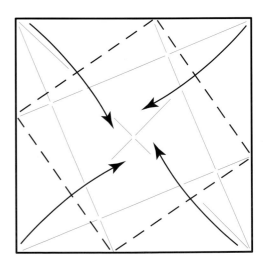

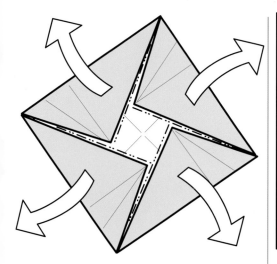

3 This will be the result. Add mountain creases that lie along raw edges. Unfold back to the square.

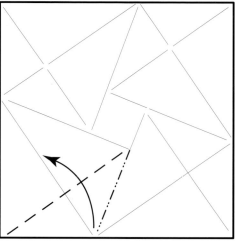

5 Start to form the paper into three dimensions, using these creases.

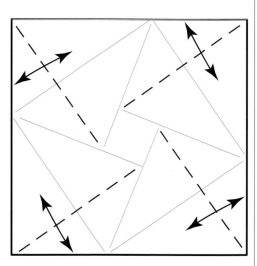

4 For clarity, some of the earlier creases are not shown on this diagram. Carefully add the four creases marked.

6 Continue on the other three sides. The small square in the centre forms the base of the pot.

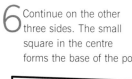

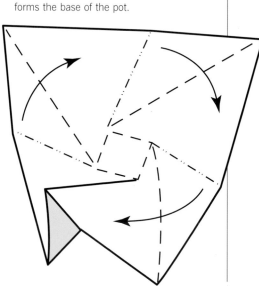

7 Fold carefully and the paper will hold quite firmly in this final position.

FLOWER

Design by Ligia Montoya
23 STEPS

Montoya was an Argentinian folder of great talent, part of the vanguard of folders who revitalized the traditional Japanese forms. Her importance as a creative folder cannot be overstated. This model is typical of her elegant designs, utilizing techniques that many other folders have since rediscovered. It requires accurate creasing and a deft touch if you start with anything other than a large hexagon. A method to create a hexagon is given first.

Paper size:
20 cm (8 in.) square
Finished flower:
10 cm (4 in.) high

FOLDING A HEXAGON

1 Starting with a square, crease both diagonals and fold in half. Add part of the upper eighth and halfway creases.

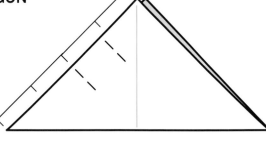

2 Fold over from the centre of the lower edge, so that the halfway crease touches the upper eighth crease.

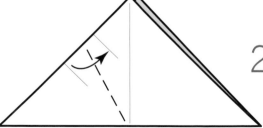

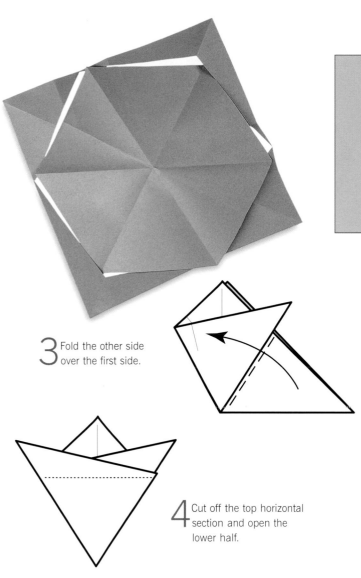

RABBIT'S EAR
REMINDER

1. Pre-crease one edge to the diagonal.

2. Repeat with the other edge.

3. Put in both creases at once.

4. Complete.

3 Fold the other side over the first side.

4 Cut off the top horizontal section and open the lower half.

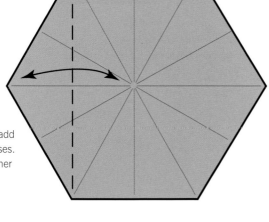

1 Start with a hexagon and add all radial creases. Fold each corner to the centre, crease and unfold.

2 Fold one corner back in.

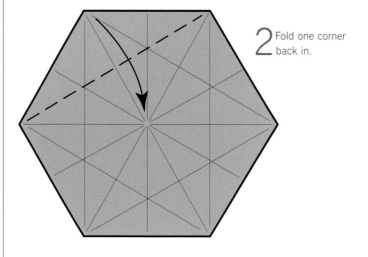

CHALLENGE
Can you find another way of forming a hexagon from a square? Use folding 60-degree angles (page 34) as inspiration.

14 Fold a flap in half, crease well, then unfold.

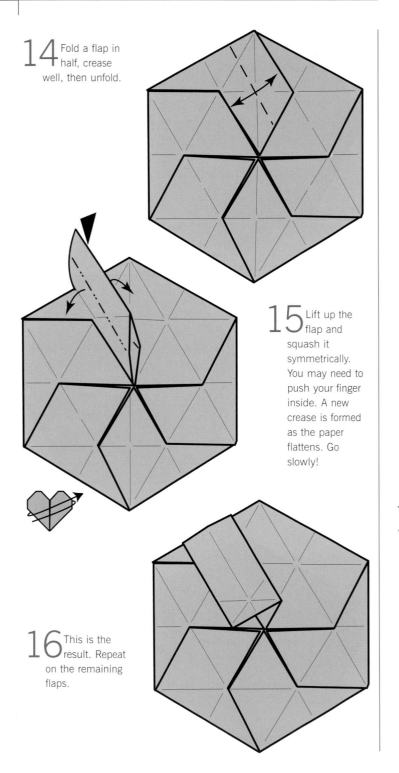

15 Lift up the flap and squash it symmetrically. You may need to push your finger inside. A new crease is formed as the paper flattens. Go slowly!

16 This is the result. Repeat on the remaining flaps.

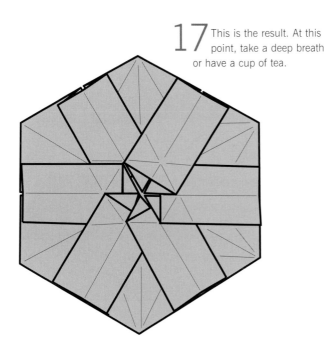

17 This is the result. At this point, take a deep breath or have a cup of tea.

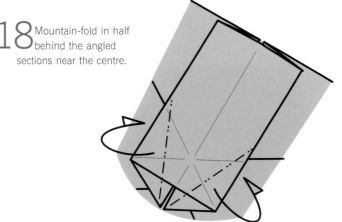

18 Mountain-fold in half behind the angled sections near the centre.

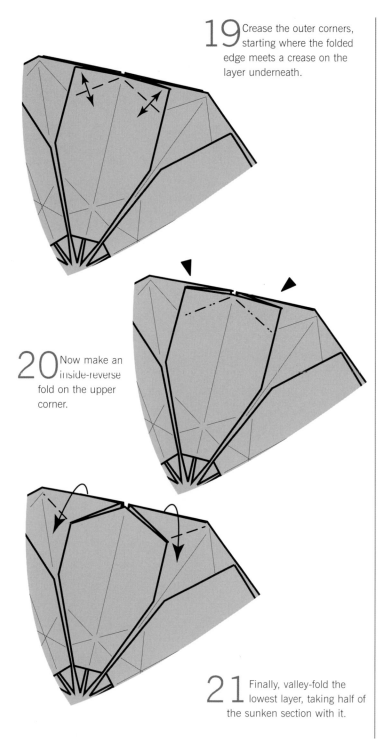

19 Crease the outer corners, starting where the folded edge meets a crease on the layer underneath.

20 Now make an inside-reverse fold on the upper corner.

21 Finally, valley-fold the lowest layer, taking half of the sunken section with it.

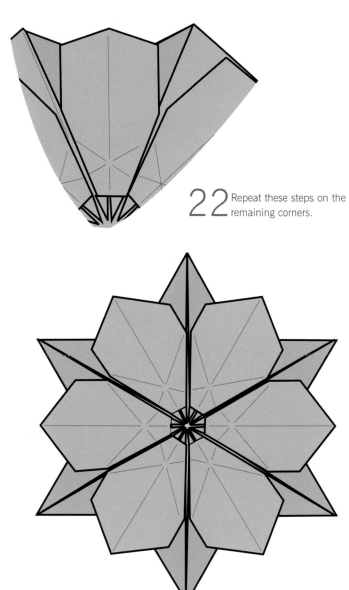

22 Repeat these steps on the remaining corners.

23 The finished model. Congratulations!

ALSO SEE

Reverse folding **page 18**

ELIAS FIGURE BASE

Design by Neal Elias

19 STEPS

Neal Elias was one of the major creative figures of the early days of American folding. During the 1960s, he developed an incredible number of designs featuring novel and adaptable techniques. One such technique is known as box-pleating, because it involves dividing the paper into a grid of boxes. This allows you to create long flaps that can be used as arms or legs. If you have enough paper, in fact, it can be used to create almost any rectilinear shape. Here are the instructions for his figure base, which recreates the basic elements of the human body. These can then be refined with smaller shaping creases, to add as much or as little detail as you require.

MULTIFORM BASE
R E M I N D E R

1. Start with a waterbomb base pattern, pre-crease each corner to the centre.

2. Fold each side to the centre, crease and unfold.

3. Completed multiform crease pattern.

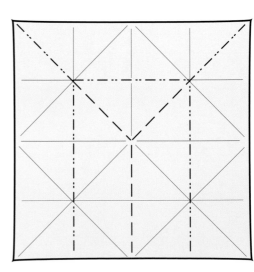

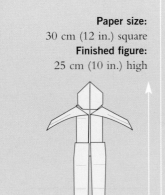

Paper size:
30 cm (12 in.) square
Finished figure:
25 cm (10 in.) high

1 Start with an unfolded multiform base (see reminder panel, above) or simply add the creases shown one at a time. Emphasize the creases and start to form the paper into three dimensions.

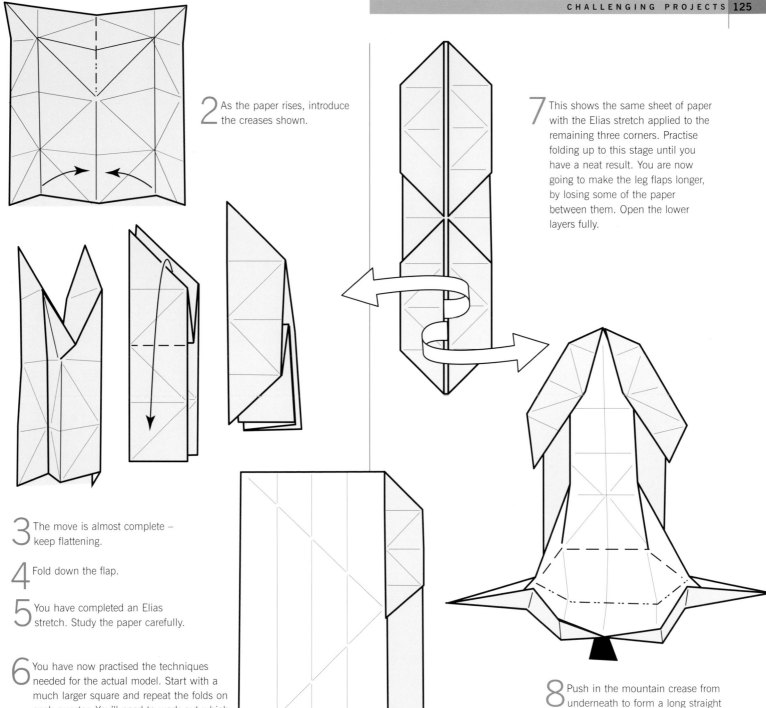

2 As the paper rises, introduce the creases shown.

3 The move is almost complete – keep flattening.

4 Fold down the flap.

5 You have completed an Elias stretch. Study the paper carefully.

6 You have now practised the techniques needed for the actual model. Start with a much larger square and repeat the folds on each quarter. You'll need to work out which creases are required. This step shows a completed quarter with some of the creases you'll need.

7 This shows the same sheet of paper with the Elias stretch applied to the remaining three corners. Practise folding up to this stage until you have a neat result. You are now going to make the leg flaps longer, by losing some of the paper between them. Open the lower layers fully.

8 Push in the mountain crease from underneath to form a long straight edge at the bottom.

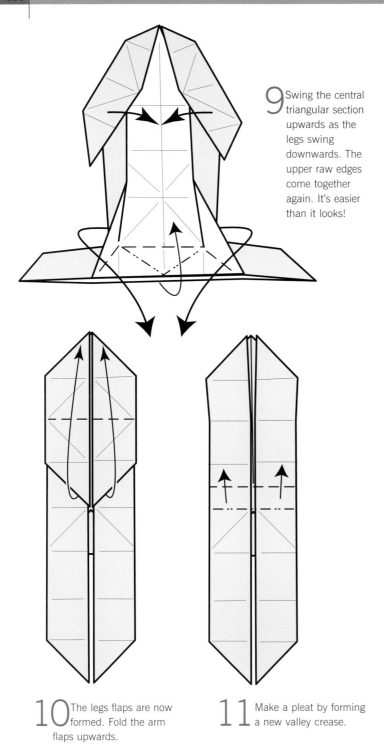

9 Swing the central triangular section upwards as the legs swing downwards. The upper raw edges come together again. It's easier than it looks!

10 The legs flaps are now formed. Fold the arm flaps upwards.

11 Make a pleat by forming a new valley crease.

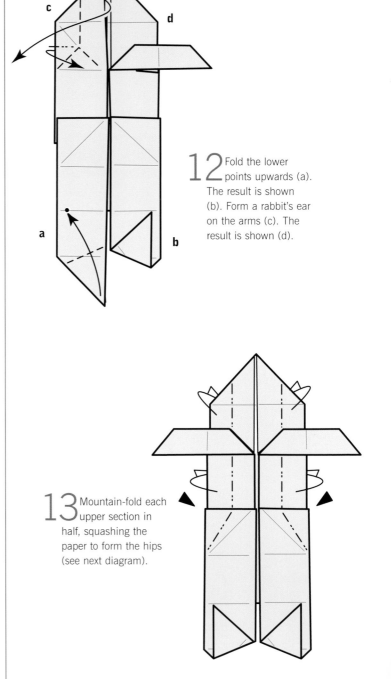

12 Fold the lower points upwards (a). The result is shown (b). Form a rabbit's ear on the arms (c). The result is shown (d).

13 Mountain-fold each upper section in half, squashing the paper to form the hips (see next diagram).

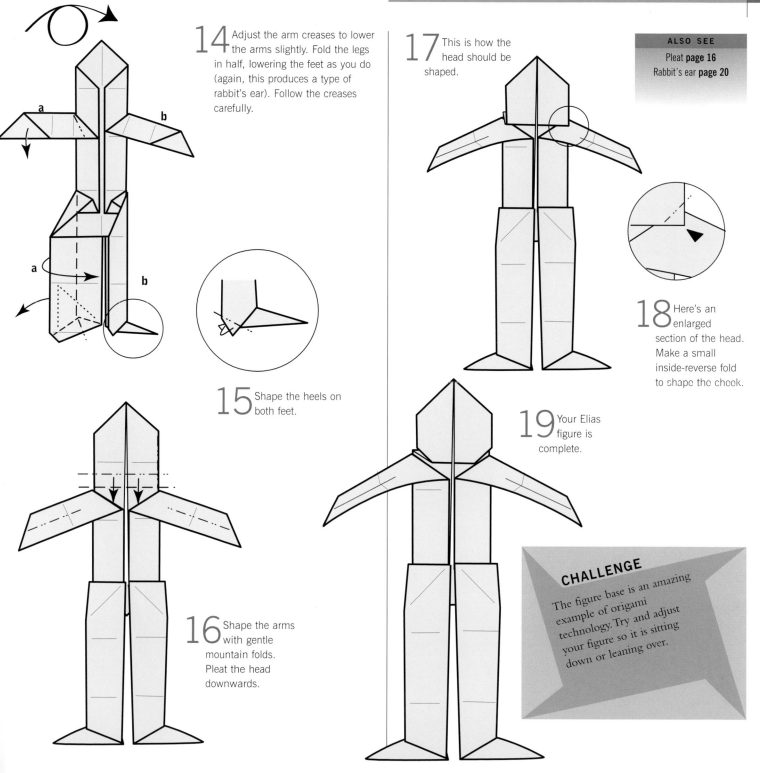

14 Adjust the arm creases to lower the arms slightly. Fold the legs in half, lowering the feet as you do (again, this produces a type of rabbit's ear). Follow the creases carefully.

15 Shape the heels on both feet.

16 Shape the arms with gentle mountain folds. Pleat the head downwards.

17 This is how the head should be shaped.

ALSO SEE
Pleat **page 16**
Rabbit's ear **page 20**

18 Here's an enlarged section of the head. Make a small inside-reverse fold to shape the cheek.

19 Your Elias figure is complete.

CHALLENGE
The figure base is an amazing example of origami technology. Try and adjust your figure so it is sitting down or leaning over.

ABSTRACT AND GEOMETRIC

Whether we realize it or not, origami has its underpinnings in geometry – we cannot escape it. The beauty of repetitive shapes and angles is undeniable. As we add more and more small units or 'modules' together, unexpected and elegant shapes appear. You'll need to fold with absolute precision for this type of design to work properly. You also need patience – many hundreds of sheets may be needed and the assembly is often complicated in the extreme, but the results are worth it!

⬑Dish: **Created by Tomoko Fuse. Folded by Joachim Gunderlach**
Four sheets of paper are woven together to form this elegant dish. While it could be made from a single sheet, the extra layers required would detract from the clean lines.

⬏ Knotologie: **Created and folded by Heinz Strobl**
Strobl has developed a technique based around knotting strips of tickertape together. These can be interwoven and combined in a near-infinite variety of forms.

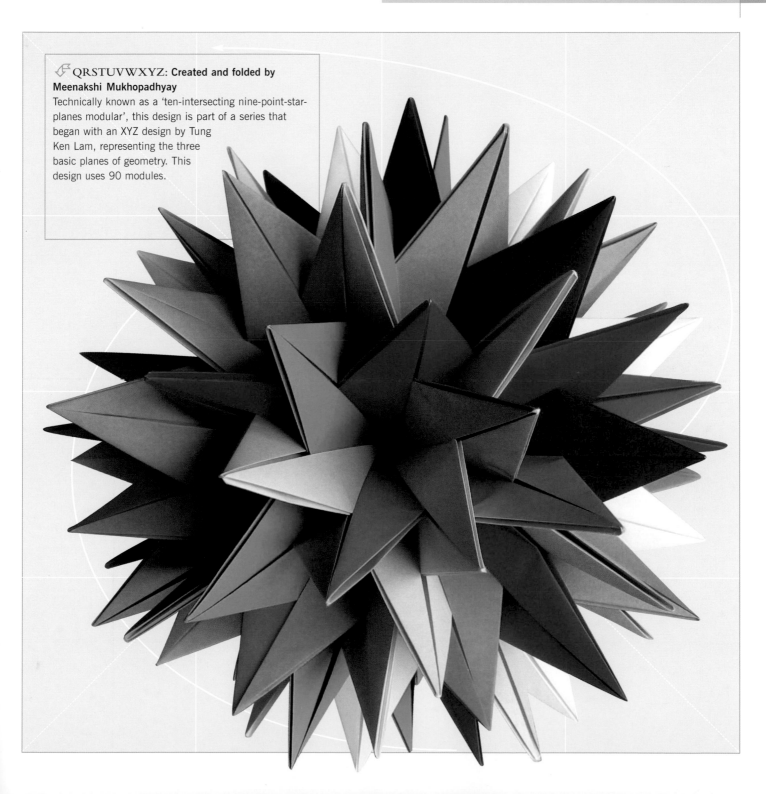

QRSTUVWXYZ: **Created and folded by Meenakshi Mukhopadhyay**
Technically known as a 'ten-intersecting nine-point-star-planes modular', this design is part of a series that began with an XYZ design by Tung Ken Lam, representing the three basic planes of geometry. This design uses 90 modules.

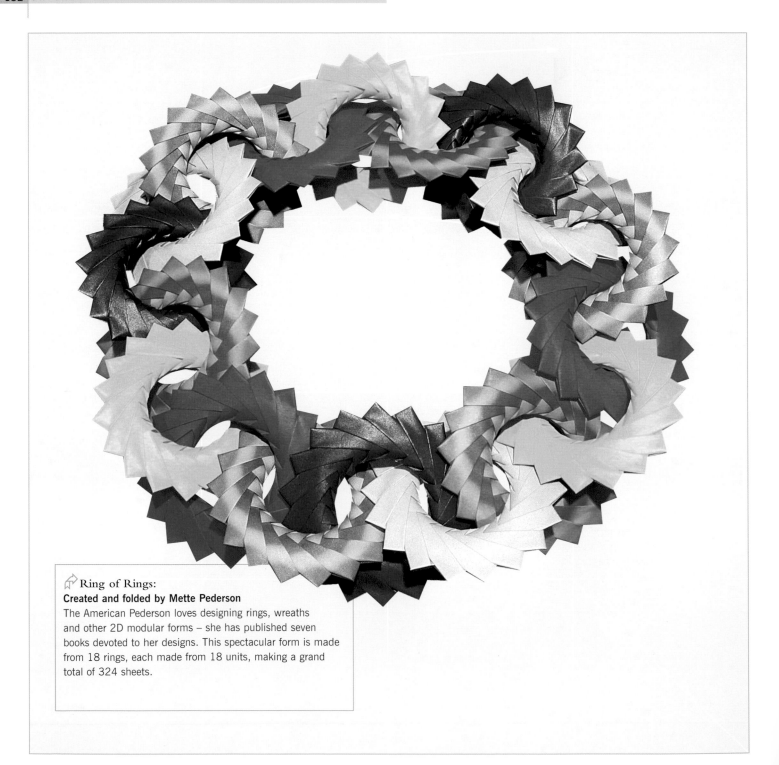

Ring of Rings:
Created and folded by Mette Pederson
The American Pederson loves designing rings, wreaths
and other 2D modular forms – she has published seven
books devoted to her designs. This spectacular form is made
from 18 rings, each made from 18 units, making a grand
total of 324 sheets.

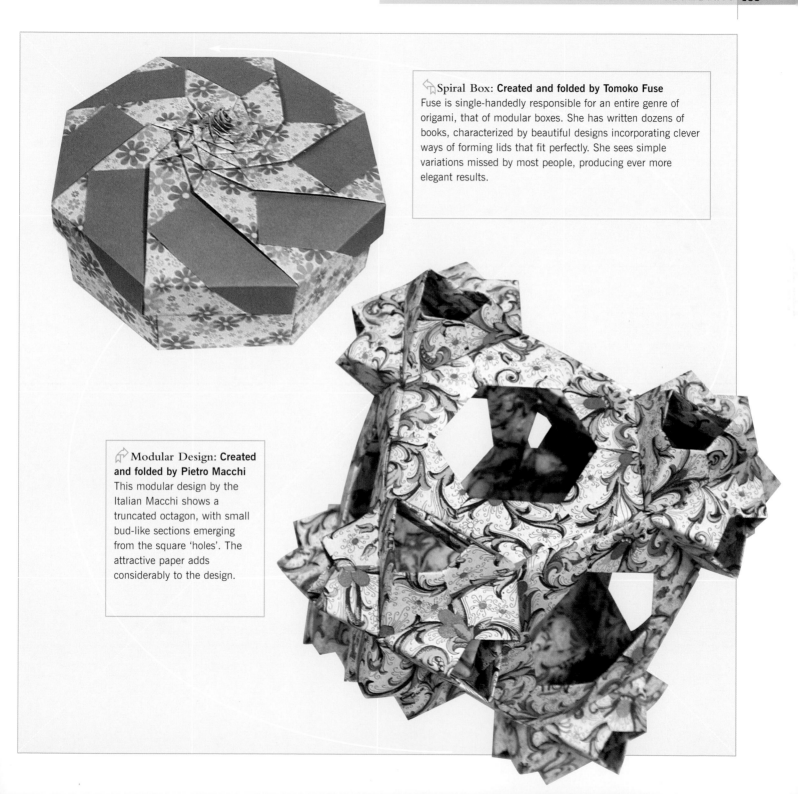

Spiral Box: **Created and folded by Tomoko Fuse**
Fuse is single-handedly responsible for an entire genre of origami, that of modular boxes. She has written dozens of books, characterized by beautiful designs incorporating clever ways of forming lids that fit perfectly. She sees simple variations missed by most people, producing ever more elegant results.

Modular Design: **Created and folded by Pietro Macchi**
This modular design by the Italian Macchi shows a truncated octagon, with small bud-like sections emerging from the square 'holes'. The attractive paper adds considerably to the design.

NATURAL AND ORGANIC

Although origami is almost always made from straight lines, the results can appear anything but straight. From a distance, many origami designs appear to be a work of nature, organic and alive. The true artist can bring life to a subject and knows how to work with the paper rather than forcing it. The choice of paper can enhance the result and give even more impressive results.

Organic Abstract: **Created and folded by Paul Jackson**
Jackson has never been afraid to break through origami barriers. For many years he has been refining and developing his work. As with many masterpieces, his works are almost impossible to reproduce.

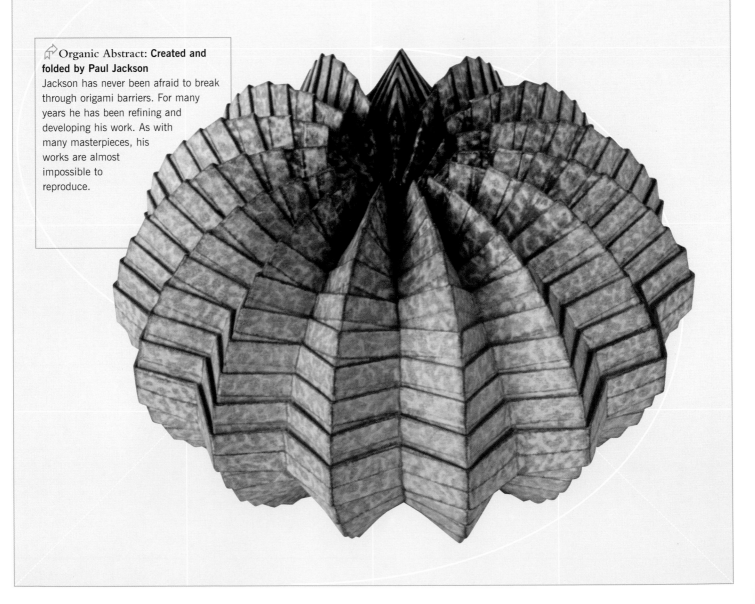

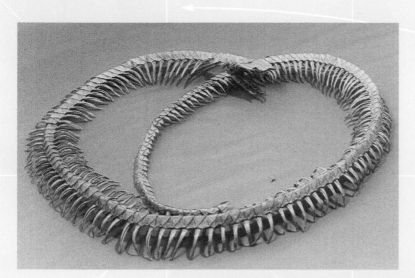

Snake's Skeleton: **Created and folded by Carlos Genova**
This design appears to be very complicated, but is in fact made from variations of the traditional bird base, cleverly locked into each other.

Shells: **Created and folded by Robert Lang**
Together with fellow American John Montroll, Lang produced a book called *Origami Sea Life*. The collections of fish, shells and other aquatic subjects represent a treasure trove of techniques for others to adapt and incorporate in their work.

FLORAL

Flowers are a popular subject, but they require sensitive folding in order to try and capture the beauty of the real thing. The more common species are often chosen as subjects. They give you an ideal opportunity to create presentation pieces incorporating leaves, stems and containers. They also make great presents!

Daffodils: **Created and folded by Mark Leonard**
Following a creative week spent with Vincent Floderer, Leonard has already begun to extend and develop the technique. These flowers have a feel that would probably be impossible without the crumpling technique.

Rose: **Created and folded by Dave Collier**
The late David Collier specialized in creating and folding flowers. This beautiful rose and stem is a fine example; simple yet elegant.

Irises in Vase: **Created by Toshie Takahama. Folded by Michael Saunders**
Takahama, the author of dozens of origami books, loved to combine simple, traditional designs with her own creations. These traditional irises with her own design of a vase and snail are a good example.

Twirl Flower with a Leaf Base: **Created and folded by Krystyna Burczyk**
This is a great example of how an initial idea can be developed by other folders. This technique for joining units together with curled flaps (initially created by Herman Van Goubergen) has been extended and taken onwards by Burczyk.

Topiary Tree: **Created and folded by John Blackman**
There is a type of Japanese design called 'kusudama', where many smaller, flower-like units are sewn together with a string to form decorative balls. This design uses a similar technique to produce an extraordinarily lifelike result, beautifully presented.

⬈ Dollar Bill Flower Pot: **Created by Herman Lau.**
Folded by Michael Saunders
This ingenious design forms both flower and pot from a single
sheet. Michael Saunders adapted the original
design to work from a dollar bill.

⬉ Butterflies on Lilies: **Created and folded by Daniel Naranjo**
This design produces a butterfly and flower from a single sheet of
paper, utilizing the different coloured sides. It has been made into
an eye-catching design by multiple examples placed on an
interesting background.

ANIMALS AND INSECTS

This subject area has probably produced more origami designs than any other. These designs range from simple, stylized versions of the chosen subject to complex, anatomically accurate renditions. All are valid and simply represent different parts of the origami spectrum.

The Sentinel: **Created and folded by Robert Lang**
Robert Lang not only creates wonderful and highly original designs, but folds them with exquisite attention to detail. The rock supporting the mountain goat is also harder to fold than it looks!

Hedgehog: **Created by John Richardson. Folded by Gilad Aharoni**
Richardson is a reclusive folder who, as far as is known, has never met another folder, yet has developed a number of amazing designs, each incorporating a startlingly new technique. This hedgehog design is over 20 years old, but still impressive.

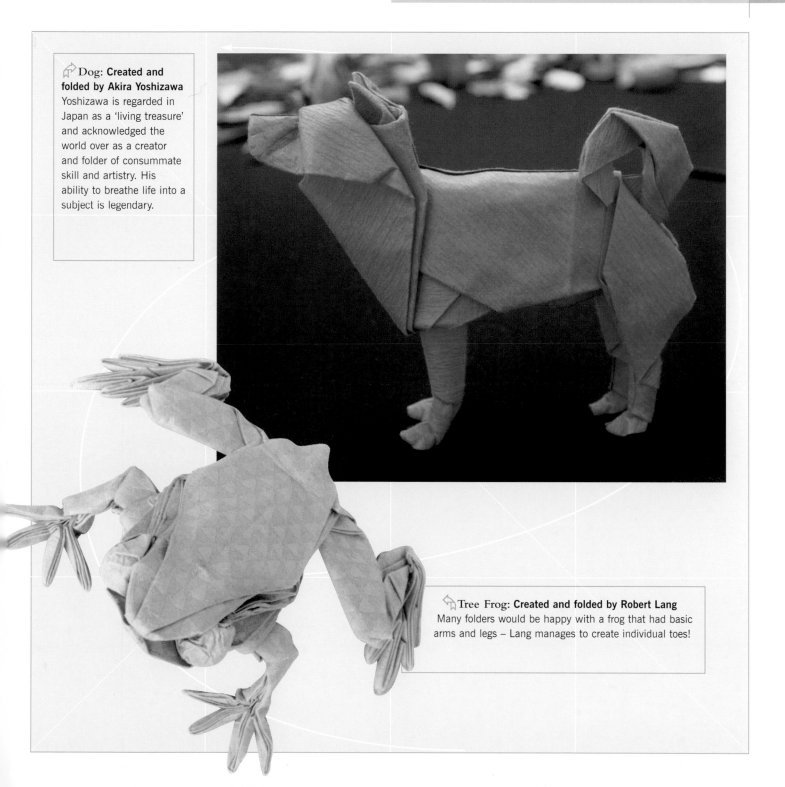

Dog: Created and folded by Akira Yoshizawa
Yoshizawa is regarded in Japan as a 'living treasure' and acknowledged the world over as a creator and folder of consummate skill and artistry. His ability to breathe life into a subject is legendary.

Tree Frog: Created and folded by Robert Lang
Many folders would be happy with a frog that had basic arms and legs – Lang manages to create individual toes!

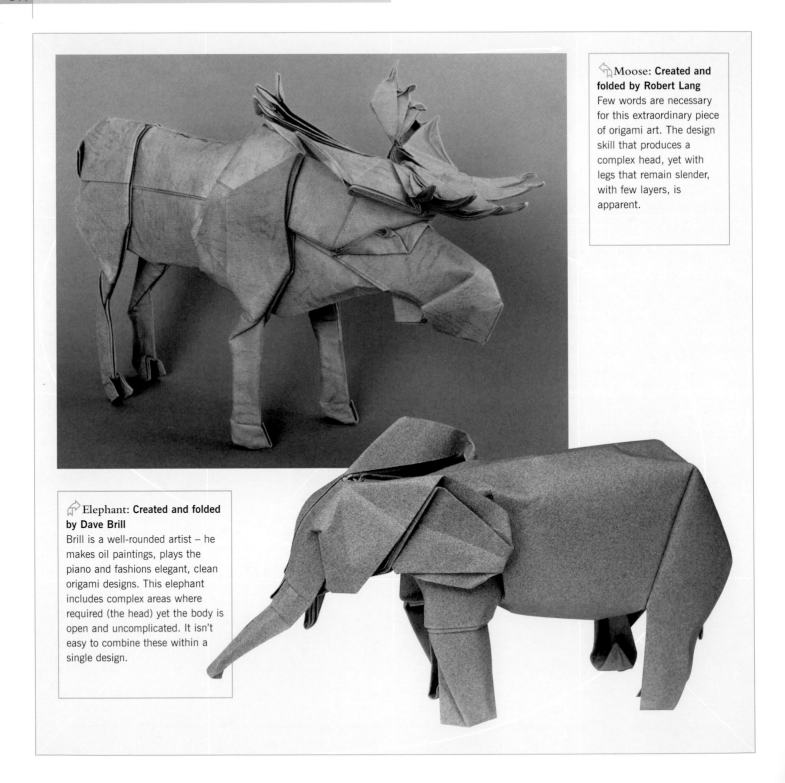

Moose: **Created and folded by Robert Lang**
Few words are necessary for this extraordinary piece of origami art. The design skill that produces a complex head, yet with legs that remain slender, with few layers, is apparent.

Elephant: **Created and folded by Dave Brill**
Brill is a well-rounded artist – he makes oil paintings, plays the piano and fashions elegant, clean origami designs. This elephant includes complex areas where required (the head) yet the body is open and uncomplicated. It isn't easy to combine these within a single design.

Squirrel: **Created and folded by Michael LaFosse**
LaFosse is a true origami artist. For his finished examples, he routinely creates a unique sheet of paper, incorporating the various paper elements (abaca, mulberry, etc) he feels will best suit the finished result. Like his mentor Yoshizawa, he breathes great life into his subjects.

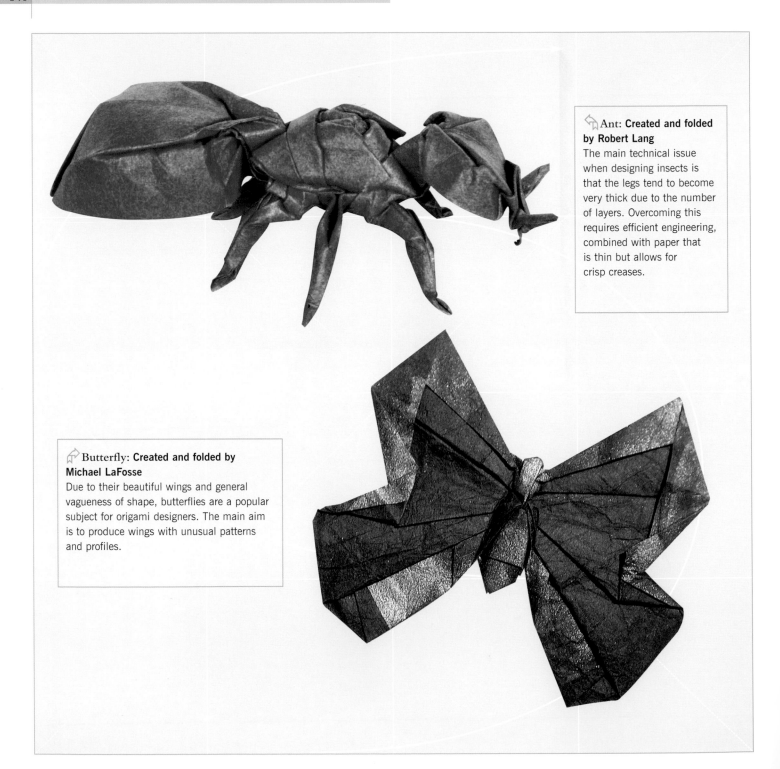

Ant: **Created and folded by Robert Lang**
The main technical issue when designing insects is that the legs tend to become very thick due to the number of layers. Overcoming this requires efficient engineering, combined with paper that is thin but allows for crisp creases.

Butterfly: **Created and folded by Michael LaFosse**
Due to their beautiful wings and general vagueness of shape, butterflies are a popular subject for origami designers. The main aim is to produce wings with unusual patterns and profiles.

Fly: **Created and folded by Alfredo Giunta**
Giunta, from Italy, has designed a remarkable collection of insects. Few folders can match his touch when attempting to reproduce these designs.

Gnat: **Created and folded by Mark Leonard**
This design requires special paper that can be moulded to produce such fine legs. It's hard to believe that it comes from a single sheet of uncut paper.

Rat: **Created and folded by Eric Joisel**
This cartoon rat is a rare example of origami that actively caricatures the subject. It is not only stylized, but also fun! Frenchman Joisel has produced some extraordinary work that is well worth seeking out.

Jackson's Chameleon:
Created and folded by Robert Lang
The wonderful design of this piece speaks for itself.

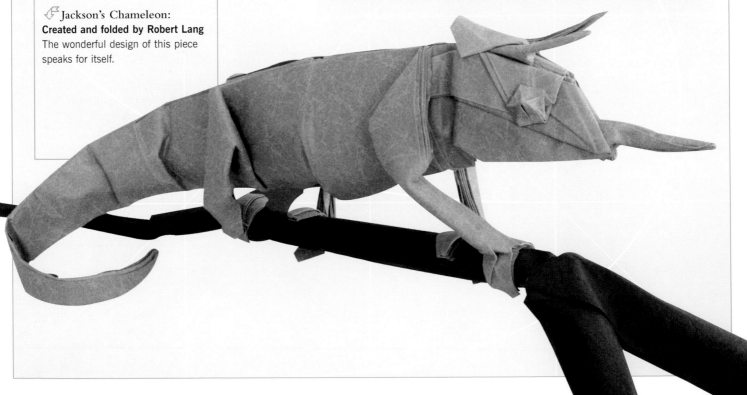

Scrub Jay on Nest:
**Created and folded by
Robert Lang**
This delightful assembly shows
how perfectly origami can
capture life.

Crab: **Created and folded by Robert Lang**
This design is fiendishly difficult to fold well – a real test of any folder's ability.

Seahorse: **Created and folded by Eric Joisel**
A magnificent example of true artistry. It seems impossible to believe that this fold isn't the real thing.

Rhino: **Created
and folded by
Stephen Weiss**
Dollar bills are perfect
for origami and the
extra paper allows the
designer to create legs
and ears with less
effort than might
be required from
a square.

Samurai Helmet Beetle:
Created and folded by Robert Lang
Another example of Lang's artistry,
giving depth and life to this
complex design.

FIGURES

Strange as it seems, the human figure is very difficult to achieve from a square of paper. This is why most origami designs in that area exaggerate proportions, or cut limbs off altogether! However, many rise to the challenge of capturing the infinite variety of the human face and form.

Devil: **Created and folded by Jun Maekawa** This design impressed everyone when it was first released in the 80s. It is still a masterpiece and represents a benchmark of folding ability – if you can make this, you are well on your way!

Ghost: **Created and folded by Carlos Genova** The only 'lifelike' part of this design is the fingers, but our imagination fills in the details and we have no trouble in accepting this as a human-like figure.

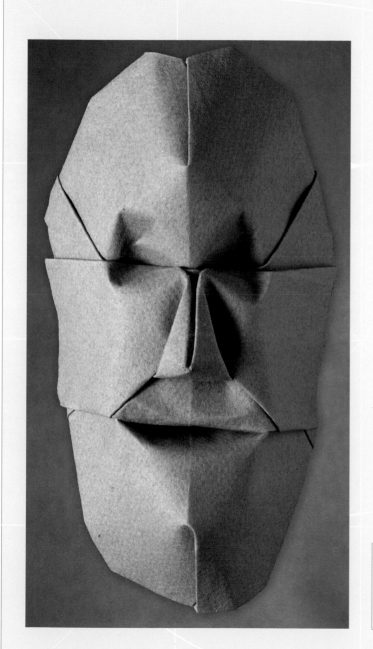

Rodin's 'The Thinker':
Created by Neal Elias
Elias was highly active during the 1960s when he developed a technique to produce arms and legs. It is still in wide use by designers today, and has become known as the 'Elias stretch'.

Mask: **Created and folded by Nick Robinson**
This mask allows for many subtleties by adjusting the shape of the eyes and mouth.

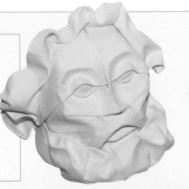

Masks: **Created and folded by Eric Joisel**
There are many origami masks around, but Joisel moved them into a different league with his range of flowing, animated creations.

Angel playing the Lute: **Created by Fumiaki Kawahata. Folded by Gilad Aharoni**
Kawahata is one of a number of Japanese folders known as the 'Tanteidan' (Detectives), who are pushing the boundaries of complex origami ever further.

 Le Victoire:
**Created and folded by
Daniel Naranjo**
Influenced by the work of
Hojyo Takashi, this design
is elegant and flowing. It
incorporates elements of
a statue rather than
literal depiction.

GLOSSARY

action model A design that does something when finished, such as a banger or paper plane.

backcoating Gluing together two different sheets (such as foil and tissue paper) to form a single sheet.

base A combination of folds that can be used as a starting point for creating a design.

bird base A classic base formed by petal-folding both sides of a preliminary base.

Blintz The technique of folding all four corners of a square into the centre.

Blintz base

box-pleating A technique developed by American folder Neal Elias in which the paper is pleated and collapsed into narrow points.

chapeaugraphy The folding of a felt ring into hat shapes.

circular origami The use of circular paper as the starting point for origami.

closed sink A sink made by gently forcing in the paper, as opposed to a standard sink made by unfolding.

collapse When a series of pre-creases are in place, you can collapse the paper into a new arrangement of layers.

crane An adaptation of the flapping bird, made by narrowing the head and tail.

crease A line formed by folding the paper.

duo Paper with a different colour on either side.

Elias-pleating See box-pleating.

flapping bird A classic design made from the bird base: a tiny bird with wings that can be made to flap.

flexagon Paper folded along regular angles in such a way that it can be turned inside out, revealing hidden faces.

foil Paper with metal foil on one side and ordinary paper on the other.

fold To bring two parts of a sheet of paper into contact, usually flattening the paper.

fold line A line used in origami diagrams to mark a fold. Dashes represent a valley fold; a dash and two dots represent a mountain fold.

folded edge An edge where two layers join.

folding geometry The angles that arise naturally (or not!) as the folding sequence progresses, such as 22.5/45/90 degrees or 30/60/90 degrees, and so on.

frog base A complex base in which each flap of a waterbomb base is petal-folded.

inverted A point or flap that has been turned inside out.

iso-area fold A fold that, when complete, displays equal amounts of front and back colour.

judgement fold A fold located by eye alone because an exact location point does not exist.

kami paper High-quality Japanese origami paper.

kite base

Kan-no-mado An ancient Japanese book showing how to fold a thousand cranes from a single sheet of paper.

kasane origami A Japanese term for layered origami in which many sheets are overlapped and arranged decoratively.

kirikomi origami A type of origami in which cuts in the paper are used to extend the range of folding possibilities of a standard origami model.

knotologie A technique for folding long strips of paper, developed by the Austrian folder Heinz Strobl.

kusudama A Japanese term for an origami ball of flowers.

location point The place on a sheet where a corner or edge must be when the fold is completed.

minimalist origami A type of origami that aims for a 'sketched' representation of the subject, usually seeking to use the minimum number of folds.

model The finished item of origami. Some folders dislike this term and use 'design' instead.

modular origami Origami in which many sheets of paper are folded into often identical units, which are then slotted together to form larger geometric designs.

module A single element of a modular design.

money-folding The use of banknotes to create origami designs.

mountain fold A crease formed by folding paper away from you and underneath. The opposite of a valley fold.

movement arrow A curved arrow used in origami diagrams to show the direction in which the paper moves.

multiform base

multi-piece origami A technique in which subjects are created from more than one sheet of paper.

one-crease origami A technique proposed by the British folder Paul Jackson, who explored the many surprising results that may be achieved by making just a single crease in a sheet.

origami A Japanese word meaning folding paper.

petal fold prepared

painting with paper A technique that uses the differently coloured sides of duo paper to represent a simple, stylized scene or subject.

petal fold A fold in which a layer is lifted up and the sides are narrowed to form a point.

pre-creases Creases that are added and unfolded, to be used later in the sequence.

preliminary base A simple and elegant base formed using 'union jack' creases.

pure origami Origami in which the paper isn't cut, glued or decorated.

pureland origami A style of origami, invented by the British folder John Smith, limited to mountain and valley folds only.

rabbit's ear A technique that forms a small triangular flap.

RAT An abbreviation meaning 'right about there', used where no location creases exist.

raw edge The edge of a single layer, one of the original outside edges of the square.

reverse fold A fold in which part of a flap is folded inside or outside another flap.

sink The paper is reversed in direction along four edges, with mountain folds becoming valley folds, for instance.

skeletal polyhedra Modular designs with paper edges and holes left where the faces would usually be.

soft crease A fold made gently so that a sharp crease isn't formed.

squash A technique in which a flap is separated and flattened, (usually but not always) symmetrically.

surface Each side of a sheet of paper.

swivel fold A technique in which paper is moved in different directions.

tessellation A design that can be tiled to form a complete pattern. Also applied to a complex method of twisting and collapsing paper.

twist-folding A technique developed by Japanese folder Shuzo Fujimoto in which pleats in the paper allow it to be collapsed into a twisted form.

union jack creases Diagonal or side-to-opposite creases.

unit origami Yunnito or modular origami.

valley fold A crease made by folding paper towards you.

washi paper High-quality handmade Japanese paper, usually containing bark from trees.

waterbomb base A simple and elegant base formed using 'union jack' creases.

wet-folding A technique invented by the Japanese paper-folder Akira Yoshizawa in which paper is dampened before folding.

yunnito origami A Japanese term for modular origami.

rabbit's ear

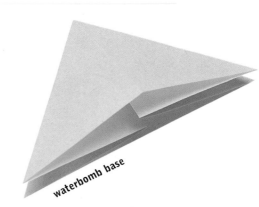

waterbomb base

INDEX

Page numbers in *italics* refer to captions

CREDITS

AUTHOR'S ACKNOWLEDGEMENTS

Special thanks to all who freely contributed designs to this book; Tomoko Fuse, Gay Gross, Giuseppe Baggi, Toe Knee O Hair, Bronco Sinkin, David Collier, Mitsonobu Sonobe, Jeff Beynon, Cristoph Mangutsch, Lore Schirokauer (her chicken transmogrified into an eagle!), Edwin Corrie, Brian Cole, Lord David Brill, Shuzo Fujimoto, Guillaume Denis, Ligia Montoya, Neal Elias and Kunihiko Kasahara. Without the generosity of creators origami books would be thin on the ground (and on the shelf). I'd better thank my family: Alison, Daisy, Nick, Morticia and Gomez Robinson for their constant carping when I don't earn money fast enough. If it wasn't for their expensive lifestyle, I wouldn't need to write books. I have many, many special origami friends, but I'd like to mention Paulo Mulatinho, Silly Schroeder, Ramin & Pepita, Andrea 'Hotlips' Thanner, Mark Robinson (who proof-read this book), Francis Ow, Bob Neale, Philip Shen, Robert and Diane Lang, Mark Kennedy and the Hazel Grove mini-meeting crew (even Ruth). Also to those special people at Origami Deutschland, Origami Vernier Genève and the Centro Diffusione Origami for recognizing talent when they see it. They have all contributed in some way to this book. Farewell to Thoki Yenn and Neil Ardley, unique individuals, much missed.

Thanks to Canson Paper and apologies to anyone I've missed.

The author uses and recommends Mesa-boogie, Marshall and Lexicon paper in his quest for origami perfection.

There are origami societies in almost every part of the world, some of which have regular magazines, conventions – where special guests visit from other countries to share their skills – or smaller, informal meetings in people's homes. Here you can fold in good company and get help with any sticky moves! The Internet is a perfect source for diagrams, photos and all kinds of origami data. Simply search for 'origami' or 'origami diagrams.' The author recommends you begin at:

www.britishorigami.org.uk

www.origami.vancouver.bc.ca

www.12testing.co.uk/origami (the author's website)

www.origami-usa.org

Whether you live in the U.K. or not, you can write to the BOS membership secretary for details of joining the British Origami Society – it has hundreds of international members and always welcomes new ones! Write to: *2a the Chestnuts, Countesthorpe, Leicester, LE8 5TL, England*

PICTURE CREDITS

Quarto would like to thank all the origami artists who supplied work for this book.
Quarto would also like to thank the following photographers of the work reproduced in this book:

(Key: l left, r right, t top, b bottom)

1, 5t, 6t, 12tr, 12bl, 132, 135t, 138l, 139, 140, 141r, 142r, 143, 144t, 145, 146t, 147t, 148, 149, 150, 151t, 153r, 154 Robin Macey 6bl, 7, 12br, 130b, 133, 136t, 137t, 138r, 144b, 146b, 147b, 151b, 152l, 153l Nick Robinson 12tl, 131 Meenakshi Mukhopadhyay 13, 134, 136b, 137b Paul Jackson 135b Paulo C. Takahashi 142l Gilad Aharoni 152r Raimundo Gadelha
All other photographs are the copyright of Quarto Publishing plc.

While every effort has been made to credit contributors, Quarto would like to apologize should there have been any omissions or errors – and would be pleased to make the appropriate correction for future editions of the book.